the
Mentoring
Mom

the Mentoring Mom

11 WAYS
TO MODEL CHRIST
FOR YOUR CHILD

By Jackie Kendall

new
hope
PUBLISHERS

Birmingham, Alabama

New Hope® Publishers
P.O. Box 12065
Birmingham, AL 35202-2065
www.newhopepublishers.com

Library of Congress Cataloging-in-Publication Data

Kendall, Jackie, 1950-
  The mentoring mom : 11 ways to model Christ for your child / Jackie Kendall.
      p. cm.
  ISBN 1-59669-005-4 (softcover)
     1.   Motherhood—Religious aspects—Christianity. 2.   Child rearing—Religious aspects—Christianity. 3. Parenting—Religious aspects—Christianity. 4. Mentoring. I. Title.
  BV4529.18.K45 2006
  248.8'431—dc22
                                     2006000203

Produced with the assistance of The Livingstone Corporation (www.LivingstoneCorp.com). Project staff includes Cheryl Dunlop and Linda Taylor.

ISBN: 1-59669-005-4

N064132 • 0606 • 7.5M1

Table of Contents

Chapter 1

THE MARK OF
the Mentoring Mom

**Principle:
A mother's example
has lifelong influence.**

W hen our kids were little, they loved to play with ink pads and stamps. Recently I came across some of our favorite old stamps. I found a much-used *Jesus Loves You* stamp. I also found a *Noah's Ark* stamp, which brought a smile to my face because it was a reminder of God's promises. No matter how bad the storm was, this stamp reminded us that God put Noah in an ark that had no rudder, no sail, and no motor and sent him into a horrible storm. Yet he was in the safest place possible, because it was God's will. Then I found my *absolute* favorite stamp: *Whatever.* That stamp came in very handy as a mom, especially during my children's teen years, because that's how you handle daily chaos—Whatever! No sarcasm was intended; rather, I was saying, "Whatever You want, Holy One...You have scripted this again."

As moms, you and I can see our lives like this: Every day we get up and get our little ink pads out, put fresh ink on our stamps, and get ready to imprint our children—and not just them, but also our husbands and lots of other people we see daily. We have the opportunity to stamp images that will be reminders to them of God's goodness, faithfulness, and love. When we do this, we become mentoring moms.

In 1984 on Mother's Day, our pastor presented the congregation with a mentoring mom challenge: "How many of you want your children to grow up to be like you?" It was a great question. I think he was trying to create a sense of conviction, but I sat there thinking, *Alright!* (I mean, minus my crazy parts.) I would *love* for my kids to be like me in the area of loving Christ. Someone once said that imitation is the highest form of flattery. Well, flattering or not, our children do imitate us. Do we as moms give our kids plenty of good things to imitate? Eventually, the life we create for our children—the habits, attitudes, daily happenings in their world—stamps their hearts with images that influence them for the rest of their lives. The single purpose of this book is to help you become a mentoring mom, one who *stamps the image of Christ* on her children.

Make Disciples

Last year my husband and I went to church with our son, Ben. His pastor, Andy Stanley, spoke about "the last thing

Jesus said before He left the earth." Now, I've got this thing about someone's last words. Don't you agree that you want to hear the words that take a person's last breath? After Jesus's death and resurrection, the last thing Jesus said is recorded in Matthew 28:19—He said, "Go and make disciples of all nations." *Make disciples* is the only imperative in that whole verse. That's the *only* one. It's like, "Listen, go make disciples." Well, when Pastor Stanley said that, I happened to have my Hebrew-Greek Bible with me, and I looked up the phrase *make disciples*. Sitting there with my head down, furiously looking, I flipped quickly through my Bible (my kids always know when they see me going fast that I'm on a trail, trying to find something).

I looked up the word *disciple*, and do you know what the first word in Greek is? *Mentor.* I thought, *Oh my goodness, mentoring is not just a 21st century cliché.* I have always thought that the word *mentor* came into vogue recently. These days, everybody talks about needing a mentor, and there are organizations to provide mentors for everyone. But Jesus Himself told His disciples to go forth and *mentor* people all over the world.

I kept looking at the word *mentor* and noticed that the very next phrase was *stamp an image.* I got so excited! Jesus called His followers to stamp an image on this world. What image? The image of Jesus Christ.

Shortly after this discovery in God's Word, I was asked to speak to some moms at a Yada Yada conference (a national conference ministry to moms and teen daughters). While on a long plane flight elsewhere, I began to ponder what I would most like to share with a group of moms. Suddenly the idea came to my mind, *How have I mentored my children?* Then immediately that question was followed by the thoughts, *What images have I stamped on the lives of my children? What do mothers stamp on children?* I got out a big legal pad and wrote out eleven images that I had stamped on my children's lives. This book is the outcome of that inspiration and a glimpse of my own heart as a mentoring mom.

I need to offer a disclaimer here. I am merely writing about my own journey. I'm not proclaiming the Ten Commandments set in stone; I'm telling what I have learned as a mom who walks with Jesus. Certainly, I would not say that I did this right every day, and I have been forgiven many times by my children—ten times more by my husband! I have a marriage that's still intact because my husband is a great forgiver and so am I. My concern is that sometimes when people hear a speaker on parenting or read books about parenting, they think there is some simple formula to follow to reach perfection as a parent. I used to hear certain speakers and think, *If I have to be that perfect, it's not going to happen.* So here I'm just sharing what I've learned so far, and, believe me, I'm still learning!

Our ability to stamp the image of Christ on others can reach outside our family circle and benefit the world around us as well. Recently, when I spoke at a retreat for students from Florida State University, I met a most inspiring woman. Her name is Lea and she has quite a burden for college students. Lea had asked herself, "How can I talk to these girls about Jesus without coming off too religious and turning them off? Who in the world wants to hear about Jesus at a party school?" Lea then brainstormed and came up with a clever way of influencing students. She opened her home for what she called "stamping parties." Girls were invited to come to her house and make beautiful gift cards for their friends and family. The girls were encouraged to make whatever they wanted because Lea had hundreds of stamps and many cool, multicolored ink pads. While the girls were stamping, painting, and decorating, Lea had chances to share the love of God with them. She is the mom of young boys, and yet she carried a burden for young girls. Her burden turned into creative mentoring. Lea was stamping an imprint of God's love by a shared activity with young women who are not her daughters.

Being a Good Mentor

Ted Engstrom, former president and chief executive officer of World Vision, wrote a five-point definition of a mentor. Every day brings opportunities for a mom to be the embodiment of these five aspects of a mentor. I matched his five points with verses that show the parallel qualities in the Proverbs 31 woman.

1. She has noble character (Proverbs 31:10).
2. She is an authority in her field as a result of work, study, and experience (Proverbs 31:26).
3. She has a certain measure of influence in her world (Proverbs 31:16–18).
4. She is genuinely interested in a protégé's growth (Proverbs 31:26, 28).
5. She is willing to commit time and emotional energy to the protégé (Proverbs 31:15–28).

Moms mentor every day; every day moms stamp lasting images on their children's hearts through their daily example. Susanne Malveaux, a CNN White House correspondent, told about the stamp of her mom on her life in the May 2003 issue of *Real Simple* magazine:

> My mom taught me purely by example. She doesn't really say, "This is what you should do." "Here is who you should befriend." "Here is who you should be kind to." She universally treats people the same. She doesn't make any class distinctions or racial distinctions—ever. People who were invited to our house for social functions when I was growing up ran the gamut. So I approach the president of the United States the same way I approach someone I meet on the street. I just don't make a distinction. That's the way my mom raised me. You say hello to everybody. You're kind to everyone. You treat everyone with the same degree of respect.

By example—that's the most effective way to make an imprint, a stamp, a lasting impression.

The following are a few of the stamps/imprints the Lord brought to mind that I want to make on my children and others; we will explore them in this book. If our children do not receive these imprints from us, they may miss the blessings that come with them. A mother can imprint on her children:

- The stamp of love for God
- The stamp of consistent prayer
- The stamp of studying God's Word
- The stamp of emotional health
- The stamp of loving people to Christ

- The stamp of your heart's passion
- The stamp of a noble life purpose
- The stamp of teachability
- The stamp of perseverance
- The stamp of reckless abandon to God
- The stamp of an adapting spouse

These are only a few of the imprints that we stamp on our children and other people each day. I am excited about using the heavenly ink pad to get plenty of ink on my stamp so that by God's grace, I can mentor many for His glory in the years ahead. Let's ink up our stamps and get out there and start imprinting people with the hope of God's awesome love.

I hope that this book will encourage you as you grow into the best mentor you can be not only for your children but also for all the people God brings into your life.

But First, Being Mentored

You may be wondering if you are capable of being a good mentor. The good news is, being a mentoring mom is a learned science, and as long as you are teachable, you will be able to stamp good images on your children's lives. Isaiah 50:4 states, "The Sovereign LORD has given me an instructed tongue, to know the word that sustains the weary. He wakens me morning by morning, wakens my ear to listen like one being taught."

From 1977 until today, I have been mentored by some of the greatest Christians who have ever lived. How did I arrange such a privilege? Let me explain. One day I was crying about my need for an older woman to encourage and mentor me. The Lord answered my cry with the coolest vision. He showed me a picture of myself sitting in my kitchen with a big glass of Diet Coke. Across from me was Elisabeth Elliot, sipping tea. He showed me that every time I read a book by a sister or brother in Christ, I am inviting the person into my home and my heart. For almost three decades, I have been mentored by some of the greatest Christians through reading their "heart in print."

The reading list in the back of this book gives you a glimpse of some of the Christians who have mentored me through the written word. If you feel like you need more mentoring yourself before you are ready to mentor your kids, some of these books may be a good place for you to start.

This Book's Plan of Action

In each chapter of this book, after a principle of stamping is presented, practical applications of the image we are to stamp will follow. The illustrations that follow each "stamped" principle are stories about our family or friends that I have taken from two decades of journaling. I know that principles without concrete examples are often hard to apply, so the journaling entries in the application sections will provide you with some concrete examples. Following the application entries, questions for group discussion are provided.

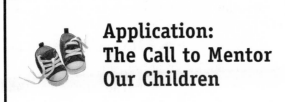

Application: The Call to Mentor Our Children

"Imitators" Compliment

Ken hates being away from his family, and the feeling is absolutely mutual with the three of us. (He is gone for four weeks leading a mission project.) During this prolonged separation, I noticed something in our children that has been such a blessing. Ben and Jessica took it upon themselves to try to fill the shoes their dad left empty. Ken is not "replaceable," but he is a pleasure to imitate.

Before we went to sleep at night, Ben would check all the doors making sure they were locked and would regulate the thermostat for comfortable sleeping. Ben kept the car *full* with gas, and the day before we went on a trip, he cleaned the car out and washed the windows. When the lights went out during a big storm, Ben immediately got the flashlights and candles while Jessica and I remained calm. Ben competently navigated our trip to LaGrange, Georgia.

Jessica imitated her dad's list-making talent. She made a list of all the pretrip preparation. She had a list for Ben, herself, and Mom. She told Ben how to pack the car most efficiently and helped him pack it. As each task was accomplished, Jessica checked it off the list. Jessica was constantly reminding Ben and me about the time and our schedules.

My mom (who went with us to Georgia) noticed how Ben and Jessica were such a great help and that they really worked as a team. I know our children are growing up, and this time without Ken shone a floodlight on their growth.

Mentors, Imitators, Mirrors

Recently we asked Ben if he would be willing to take care of his sister while we were away. His response, "Absolutely. Just get me her schedule so I will know what she needs." When we returned, we discovered not only that Jessica was well cared for, but also that some parental modeling had been imitated: Ben had written Jessica encouraging notes that greeted her when she awoke, and Jessica had written notes of appreciation for the TLC her brother was so willingly giving her.

Ken and I have been writing each other cards and love notes for more than 24 years. We have also written our children love notes ever since they could read. How precious to see the legacy continuing. Love notes are wonderful deposits for a person's love tank!

A Mom and a Mentor

When I was 19 years old, I regularly talked to Mamie, a woman who was 50ish. I confided in her the process of my journey as a young Christian, and she listened and then responded with God's Word. She always matched my circumstances or my struggles with Scriptures. She was someone else's mom, but she was my spiritual mom and my first mentor.

Yesterday I was sharing Scriptures with a precious 18-year-old girl, and I reflected back to the countless conversations I had with Mamie at that age. I realized that as I neared the age of 50, I was doing the same thing that Mamie had done with me three decades ago. Whenever this 18-year-old girl calls me, I listen to her and then I share the appropriate Scriptures for her situation. My joy was doubled as I realized that I am not only this 18-year-old's mom but I am presently her mentor, too.

Ken and I have always seen discipleship as a normal part of parenting. Today I am humbled by the reality that I am allowed for this present time to be a mentoring mom.

Jessica told her dad the other night, "All I want to do, Dad, is to be like Mom—a wife, mom, and Bible teacher." When Ken told me her remark, I cried and felt like I had been given an early 50th birthday gift!

How About Mentoring Me, Mom?

Several young women have approached me about spending time with them this summer in a mentoring setting. As I have prayed about it, I only had peace about one particular young woman. Then I got a phone call from Jessica. She said, "Mom, how would you feel about me coming home and spending time with you this summer, like in a mentoring relationship? I can also help Dad at World Servants." Her request moved to first place in my schedule and heart. My prayer for her this summer is that she would grasp the reality of Oswald Chambers' famous remark: "One life wholly devoted to God is of more value to God than one hundred lives simply awakened by His Spirit."

Welcome home, Jessi!

Mentoring Journey Update

A young woman named Sami has begun work on a doctorate. She came to interview me on the subject of older women mentoring younger women. I started describing the journey that Jessica and I have been on this summer. She wanted to know if we were doing a particular study together. I told her that besides our quiet times, we were reading and discussing the following books:

- *Following Christ,* by Joseph Stowell
- *A Hunger for God,* by John Piper
- *Spiritual Classics,* edited by Richard Foster and Emilie Griffin

When Jessi was a little girl I used to read to her daily, and it was one of my favorite times as a mom. Now that she is a young woman, we read the same books, and we share what touches our hearts. So often when Jess comes into my room to read a quote from one of the books we are reading, I just grin because I have highlighted the same quote. What a privilege to fan the flames of her passion to have a white hot love for her Lord! I know that this time with Jessica this summer is an exceptional moment and I am so grateful.

When Jesus instructed His disciples to "make disciples," He knew that such mentoring would be passing the torch of truth and hope to future generations. Such mentoring would allow the one mentored to share in the life as well as the truth that Jesus embodied. What more important gift can you give to your children? May God bless your family as you mentor the next generation in the way of Christ!

Questions:
For Individual Reflection
or Group Study

1. In what ways do you want your children to grow up to be like you?
2. What does the word mentor mean to you?
3. Do you think of yourself as a mentor to your children?
4. How does the idea of mentoring change the way you view your role as a mom?
5. Who are the people in your life who have mentored you in Christ? In what ways would you like to imitate them?

Chapter 2

STAMP THE IMAGE OF
Love for God

 **Principle:
Love for God comes first.**

The first stamp that I wanted to "ink up" and stamp on my children and their friends was the image of love for God. How does a mother stamp the image of love for God on anyone? How does a mother know that she loves God, and how does she know whether she displays such love? One of the first aspects of love for God is responding to being loved by God. I know a lot of women who do not know the depth of God's love for them. Oh, they have heard about His love, and they have seen little stickers that say "God loves you." They can sing songs about His love, but the experiential aspect of being loved by God and loving Him proportionately is often lacking. After spending time with a woman, I can tell whether or not she knows how deeply loved she is by God.

What keeps a mother from knowing the depth of God's love for her? What keeps her from inking up the stamp of the image of love for God? I have observed two very common reasons that a mom does not know how deeply God loves her. The first is that she does not have a clear picture of God's love for her; the second is that she is not spending time remaining in that love. When I say that a mom does not have a clear picture of God's love, I am not talking about a picture of Jesus or of the cross; I am talking about a clear view of God's heart for her personally or specifically. I read an illustration last summer that absolutely convinced me of our inadequate view of the glorious One who is so in love with us.

There is no more wonderful image in nature of the glory of God than we find in the starry heavens. Telescopes have long discovered the wonders of God's universe. By means of photography, new wonders of that glory have been revealed. A photographic plate fixed below the telescope will reveal millions of stars which otherwise could never have been seen by the eye. The stars, at first wholly invisible, will leave their image on the plate. The plate must be exposed for several hours to receive the full impression of the farthest stars. (*Spiritual Classics*, edited by Richard Foster and Emilie Griffin, p. 272)

Our hearts are like the photographic plate of those sophisticated telescopes—the picture of the reflection of God's love takes *time* to be produced. To capture the full expression of God's wonderful love for you, you must take time each day to catch a glimpse of Him. When a busy mom takes time for God by reading His Word and praying, the image of God's love is photographed more clearly on the plate of her heart. Prolonged time allows the photographic plate to capture clearer pictures of the stars. The more time a woman spends with God, the clearer her impression and view of God's love will be.

Every day when I spend time with Jesus, I get another snapshot of His love on my photographic plate. When I meet a mother who is unsure of the depth of God's love, I wonder how much time she spends allowing the photographic plate of her heart to be exposed to the starry light of God's love. Abraham Lincoln said that the greatest gift to mankind besides Jesus Christ was the Word.

One day while reading God's Word—allowing my photographic plate to be exposed for another impression of the Holy One—I found an illustration of His love that spurred the creation of the *"Jedidiah Cult."* Let me explain before you report me to the authorities.

The Jedidiah Cult

One day the Lord gave me such a wonderful new message:

> Then David comforted Bathsheba, his wife, and slept with her. She became pregnant and gave birth to a son, and they named him Solomon [peaceable]. The LORD loved the child and sent word through Nathan the prophet that his name should be Jedidiah—"beloved of the LORD"—because the LORD loved him. (2 Samuel 12:24–25 NLT)

As I thought about the phrase "beloved of the LORD," I immediately thought of the angel in Daniel who referred to Daniel as one who was "greatly beloved" of the LORD (Daniel 9:23 NKJV). *Beloved* in Hebrew refers to being "delectable." As I continued to meditate on the name Jedidiah, this next thought came to mind: "Jackie, in Jesus you are Jedidiah." As my heart began to leap with joy, I remembered another verse in the New Testament that describes this "Jedidiah love": "I'm not saying I will ask the Father on your behalf, for *the Father himself loves you dearly* because you love me and believe that I came from God" (John 16:26–27 NLT, italics added).

As the joy in my heart was reaching the bursting level, the Lord gave me a chance to share this thought at my Tuesday Bible study. The day that I was born again and I began my love affair with Jesus, I became "Jedidiah— beloved of Yahweh." I have been running around boldly sharing that we are "Jedidiah" because of the lavish love that has been poured out on us in Jesus (1 John 3:1).

For nine days, I have been pretty focused on the blessing of being "Jedidiah because of Jesus." Then I told a few friends that I was going to start the Jedidiah Cult, and they all thought I was completely crazy until I explained the definition of a cult. *Cult* means an "obsessive devotion to a person, principle or ideal." When I read that definition, I began squealing with joy because I am absolutely obsessed and devoted to Jesus, His principles, and His ideals (the Word). I shared this idea with our daughter and she said, "Mom, I just recently learned in class that what distinguishes a cult as negative is the unworthy object of focused obsession and devotion."

Only Jesus is worthy of such obsessed devotion, and those who know they are "Jedidiah in Jesus" will want to be honorary members of the Jedidiah Cult.

The next time you are feeling a little unloved or unappreciated, just say out loud the Hebrew name Jedidiah. Consider this whether you are in a grocery store, an elevator, doctor's office, school sports event, or your kitchen—wherever you are, you can say the name Jedidiah and therefore remind yourself of the truth that you, because of Jesus, are loved by the incomparable, only God, Yahweh. *Yahoooo!*

> His unchanging plan has always been to adopt us into his own family by bringing us to himself through Jesus Christ. And this gave him great pleasure. (Ephesians 1:5 NLT)

As an honorary member of the Jedidiah Cult, I am grinning over the reality that it was *God's decision,* which He deemed best (*pleasure,* in Greek) to pick you and me to be adopted into His forever family. Now if that doesn't crank your tractor and cause your heart to want to cry out, "I am Jedidiah in Jesus!," then we may have to postpone your honorary membership in the Jedidiah Cult.

This is just one illustration of God's profound love for us. A dear friend sent me some lapel pins that read: "Jedidiah Is for Lovers."

When you understand how much God loves you, you carry the nickname of "Jedidiah." A woman with this nickname is ready each day to ink up her "Love for God" stamp and stamp away on the lives of the people who surround her.

Remaining in Jesus's Love Forever

I mentioned that I have seen two reasons that a mother doesn't grasp the love of God. The first reason was a lack of knowledge and experience with God's love. The second reason is explained by Jesus in a most familiar passage.

> "As the Father has loved me, so have I loved you. Now remain in my love." (John 15:9)

How does a mother remain in the love of the Jesus? How does a mother wake up daily with the confidence that she is ready to ink up her stamp and continue mentoring those who she loves? Jesus answers the *how to remain in His love* question in the very next verse:

> "If you obey my commands, you will remain in my love, just as I have obeyed my Father's commands and remain in his love." (John 15:10)

My obedience acts as a guard over the love between Jesus and me. The word *remain* is defined in a Greek lexicon as "warden, guard, keep an eye on." So you and I keep an eye on God's love through our daily obedience.

Recently we were discussing with Ben how much obedience is linked to trust. We began to discuss how obedience is part of a trinity—love, trust, and obedience. They are inextricably linked together. "But you rebelled against the command of the LORD your God and refused to trust him or obey him" (Deuteronomy 9:23 NLT). Then Ben said, "Mom, the simple prefix of *dis* means to shrink." So *dis*obedience is the shrinking of obedience. Then I realized that when trust shrinks, disobedience occurs and this impacts the love we are to be guarding—*remain in My love*.

So if you are struggling as a mom to obey Jesus in a specific area, consider the reality that the struggle has been intensified by the shrinking of your trust in His love for you. Dietrich Bonhoeffer demonstrated with his life the reality of obedience that reflects one's trust and, in turn, reflects one's belief. He died for what he believed about the love of God. Such a strong belief is captured in one of his famous remarks: "Only he who believes is obedient; only he who is obedient believes." The call to obey is simply a call to display what you as a woman believe about God's love for you. If you are struggling, it is time to find time for your photographic plate to be exposed again to the starry brilliance of God's love for you. Remember, to know God is to love Him. Time spent with Him only intensifies your ability to *keep an eye on* the love of God.

Who was the last person on whom you stamped the image of God's love? Do your children know with absolute assurance that their mom is a student of God's love? Do your children know that you are trusting and obeying God because you are so in love with Him?

> This is love for God: to obey his commands. And his commands are not burdensome, for everyone born of God overcomes the world. This is the victory that has overcome the world, even our faith. (1 John 5:3–4)

Notice the trinity in this verse: love, obey, and faith (trust).

Recently I received a letter from a young woman who had met our son Ben and wanted to tell me something Ben had shared at a singles fellowship dinner. The single adults were discussing the hobbies and interests of their parents. This young woman wrote about Ben's description of his mom's activities. "Your son said to us, 'Most people have hobbies or are identified by interests and passions, but my mom is just interested in Christ. Her hobbies are witnessing and praying.'" The young woman went on to say, "I long to be a woman who is described with the words that Ben used." All my son was doing was exposing his heart that had been stamped by his mom's "Love for God" stamp.

God's Word has absolutely convinced me that God is crazy about me. In response to God's love for me, I have become a God chaser. "I remember the devotion of your youth, how as a bride you loved me and followed me through the desert" (Jeremiah 2:2). The more we grasp how much we are loved by God, the more freely we can respond in love for God. Now ink up your "Love for God" stamp and get out there and start stamping people with love for God!

Application: The Stamp of Love for God

A Most Precious Bouquet of Flowers

Last week we had the privilege of taking Ben with us to a PAO conference where he not only could see our ministry together, but he also was able to hear one of the most unbelievable speakers we have ever heard. He is Brennan Manning (a former Catholic monk), and he understands the love of God on a level that leaves the listener wondering, *Will I ever believe that God loves me that much?* In fact, one night Ben and I sat up till 1:00 A.M. discussing why it is so hard to believe that God is so in love with us.

A Big Brother's Gift

Since Jessica was in first grade, Ben has been giving her tips on self-defense. So many times I would hear Ben telling Jessica what to do in case some boy bothers her. I have always smiled and enjoyed Ben's protective attitude. Sometimes when Ben would be trying to show Jessica how to defend herself, she would tell him, "I don't need any more instruction."

Well, Ben's "big brother's gift" paid off recently. Jessica was at a friend's 13th birthday party, and our friend Bob observed the following situation (which he shared with me the next day at church). Jessica was talking to a friend when a boy she did not know came up to her from behind and began to tickle her. Her first response, "Please stop doing that!" Then, when he tried again, she responded, "Don't do that again, if you know what's good for you!" Bob had to control his urge to laugh as he watched Jessica firmly handle this boy's advances. I told Bob that her brother had helped Jessica develop this secure boundary.

The Kendall Love Feast

Parenting a Junior Varsity cheerleader takes us to the JV games and parenting a Varsity football player takes us to all the Varsity games. Dad and Mom are in the stands cheering and supporting them. Our favorite time "out of the stands" with our teens is eating a meal together afterwards. Have you seen the TV commercials encouraging families to eat meals together? For us, these "dining together" times have proven to be invaluable for keeping the lines of communication open between our foursome. The Kendall love feast seems to be a great bridge spanning the generation gap.

Fanning the Flame for Jesus

The night of Ben's high school graduation, he told us to watch for a "special signal" when he walked up for his diploma. Knowing the wild man our Ben can be, I was a little nervous. After Ben received his diploma, we saw him put two fingers together, place them on his lips, and throw a kiss to the crowd. The significance of the kiss-throwing gesture is that Jessica always ends her big cheering stunts with the same fun gesture. Ben using Jessica's gesture was just another tender reminder of his love and respect for his little sister. Our foursome has learned how to be "fans" of one another in love.

The Beloved of the Lord

While Ben was doing an internship in Jacksonville, he lived with friends of ours. One day, little Harry was waiting for Ben to return from work, and when Ben drove up, Harry (6) asked Ben (21) if they could swing on the hammock together and watch the sunset. Ben told Harry he would meet him out back after he changed out of his work clothes. As they lay there on the hammock watching the sunset, Harry rolled over on Ben's chest and began staring intently at Ben's mouth. Ben asked Harry, "What are you doing?"

"I am wanting to inhale the air you exhale," Harry replied.

Tears came to Ben's eyes when he told me the story, because it reminded him of the verse we framed for Ben on his special weekend of blessing when he was 13 years old. The Lord longs for such intimacy with us as Harry and Ben shared that day on the hammock: "Let the beloved of the LORD rest secure in him, for he shields him all day long, and the one the LORD loves rests between his shoulders" (Deuteronomy 33:12). As the Holy One exhales, we inhale.

I Was Thinking About You

Recently while Jessica and I were running some errands, she asked if she could have some French fries from Checkers. I agreed, and as I drove up to order her fries, Jessica said, "Why don't we get Ben a vanilla milk shake; he likes them so much!" I was touched by Jessica's thoughtfulness. When we walked into the house, Jessica shouted, "Ben, we have a surprise for you!"

Ben said, "I've got a bigger surprise for you, Jessica!" While Jessica and I were running errands, Ben was channel-surfing on the TV and saw the National Junior High Cheerleading Championships and taped them for Jessica. Ben knows how much our resident cheerleader loves to watch cheering competitions.

My eyes filled with tears as I thought about the way Ben and Jessica had spontaneously thought of each other. Sometimes when they are bickering I think they hate each other, but the Lord reminds me of the many times when they are thinking about each other unselfishly. Ken and I have desired that Ben and Jessica actually enjoy each other rather than endure each other. I think they are learning how to really love each other. Two weeks ago, Ben's friend Vincent told me, "You can really tell that Ben loves his little sister." This young man has only seen Ben and Jessica at school, yet he was able to catch a glimpse of their love for each other. I am so jazzed because I was never close to any of my siblings as a teenager (and I had six siblings). I have prayed and worked with our kids in the area of their honoring and loving each other. They regularly heard paraphrases of 1 John 4:20, "If anyone says, 'I love God,' yet hates his brother, he is a liar. For anyone who does not love his brother, whom he has seen, cannot love God, whom he has not seen."

Learning to love each other has not eliminated skirmishes between Ben and Jessica, but the love has become a secure boundary around their relationship.

Africa Beats Again in Ben's Heart

This morning, Ben had the privilege of speaking for the student chapel at Wellington Christian School. Our staff member from Africa, Gracie Kalute, asked Ben if he would come with her and tell the students about his trip to Africa. What a blessing to hear Ben share about his awesome adventure with God in Africa. My smile was so big my cheek bones almost got a Charlie horse! One of the students asked Ben what his qualifications were to go to Africa, and Ben answered, "A heart full of love and a willingness to work are the only qualifications." Gracie told the students that Ben was willing to do the "not-so-nice jobs." She also told the students the Africans were so surprised that a teenager (only 14) would come all the way to Africa to serve Jesus.

A teacher asked why Ben went to Africa. His response was, "My dad presented me with the opportunity and, after praying about it, I knew that the Lord wanted me to go and display in Africa the love I have for Jesus that I try to show through my words and actions here in America."

As I drove Ben to school after he had finished speaking, he put his hand over his heart and said, "After speaking about Africa, my heart is beating again for Africa. Mom, I think I might need to go again this summer."

I told him that we would wait and see what the Lord wanted from him. I reminded him that he has already begun preparing with our church youth group for a mission trip with World Servants to the Dominican Republic. In fact, to go on this particular trip, Ben had to join the youth choir, which for him was a most heroic deed!

Holy Hugs: Double-Stuffed Oreos

We are a family of huggers. We hug when we say hello and we hug when we say good-bye. Our niece Kelly shared with us a funny remark that her new hubby, Rob Wilson, made concerning his first impression of meeting the Kendall gang. Whenever you enter a Kendall home, everyone lines up and the hugging begins. When you say you need to go, they form a "reception line" to begin the good-bye hugs.

This remark caused me to burst into laughter, because throughout our kids' lives, we have always emphasized hugging and saying, "I love you." Our children are comfortable with the concept of intimacy with God because of the intimacy they experienced in our home. We had a code for our holy hugs; we called them "double stuffed Oreos." We would do a group hug, kids in the middle and Ken and me on the outside, and the kids would say, "We are the stuffing and Mom and Dad are the chocolate cookies!"

In 1991 I heard David Seamands teach on the distorted concept of God that keeps so many Christians in bondage. The home is the first glimpse our children get of the concept of being loved by God. If they are not secure in our love for them, how will they ever comprehend the Father of the universe loving them? Holy hugs in the frame of "double-stuffed Oreo cookies" were significant in our kids' foundational concept of being loved by their heavenly Abba (Galatians 4:6).

Lynda Bell Gilliam, author/songwriter from Dallas, said: "Always let your children know that they are loved. Tell them every day. Kiss them and let them know that you consider them to be your greatest gifts" (*Real Simple* magazine, May 2003).

A Most Affordable Christmas Gift

Here is a story from *Connecting* by Larry Crabb:

> In a conversation with Brennan Manning, I impulsively blurted out, "Brennan, I want time with you to talk seriously about something in my life. I need your help." Always gracious, Brennan

immediately agreed. I wondered what had triggered that unplanned spontaneous request.

As I reflected on my plea for help, two memories returned. Several years earlier, Brennan had told me of his spiritual director's curious habit. Whenever he saw Brennan after an extended absence, he jumped up and down with delight. I remember smiling. I pictured an elderly gentleman walking down a deserted beach toward an agreed upon meeting point and, spotting Brennan from a distance, hopping three or four times. The image amused me. It also drew me.

A year later, my wife Rachael and I tumbled out of a crowded elevator into a hotel lobby teeming with conference participants. Across the way, I caught a glimpse of Brennan's white hair and unmistakable smile. As I leaned toward Rachael to tell her I had just seen Brennan, he turned and saw us. Immediately, he jumped up and down. I was warmed to the bottom of my heart. When those two memories returned, I understood my unexpected plea for help. *I could trust a man who delighted in me.*

That story just rocked my world. Am I the kind of person who hops for joy when I see a brother or sister? Do I see the good in people? A good heart is sometimes buried under pettiness, resentments, and empire-building, which irritate me. Do I accept fellow Christians the way Christ accepts me, forgiving others for the wrongs they do and believing there is something better?

God's Job Description: Awesome

Both of our kids are home this summer from college. Yahoo! Ben is taking ten hours in summer school, and Jessica is going to be a camp counselor. The noise and laughter have returned, and so have Ben's classic one-liners. The other day when Ben and I were driving somewhere and I was sharing something incredible God had done for a dear friend, I said, "God is so awesome." Ben immediately responded, "That is why He got the job!"

Questions:
For Individual Reflection
or Group Study

1. Discuss the comparison between the telescope and the photographic plate of your heart. (2 Corinthians 3:17-18; Romans 8:28-29)
2. Share what has convinced you of God's deep love for you. (1 John 3:1; 4:10; Romans 8:31-32, 37-39)
3. Respond to Jesus's remark in John 15:10: "If you obey my commands, you will remain in my love." (John 14:15, 23)
4. Discuss the concept of the Jedidiah Cult. (1 Samuel 12:24, 25; Jeremiah 2:2)
5. Consider the parallels between obedience and trust. (Deuteronomy 9:23; 1 John 5:3-4)

Chapter 3

STAMP THE IMAGE OF
a Praying Woman

 **Principle:
Prayer is life's
greatest work.**

When my husband and I were dating as poor college students, we often went for walks on our dates. Near our campus was a railroad track that no longer was in use. We often walked that railroad track, and we would "prayer walk" during part of the time. Ken and I were taking "prayer walks" long before that was an in-vogue expression. Sometimes we would be walking along talking to God when another student approached us. We always said, "Excuse us Father; we'll be back in a moment." Then we greeted the other student(s) and chatted for a moment. After the interruption, Ken and I would continue walking and praying.

Ken and I did not pray together as a couple to impress others with our spirituality. Ken and I prayed together as a couple because we enjoyed talking to the One who loved us more than we would ever love each other. We knew that God had brought us together as journey partners, and a very common aspect was prayer. In fact, right after Ken and I consummated our love on our wedding night, Ken started talking to the One who created such intimacy. "Marriage should be honored by all, and the marriage bed kept pure" (Hebrews 13:4). When Ken started praying, I realized how much he understood what a holy moment it was. Now Ken and I have been married for 30 years, and that first night's practice of talking to Abba Father before going to sleep has been as common for us as brushing our teeth before going to bed.

Some people think that prayer is preparation for a great work, but I think prayer is the greatest work. As a mother, this is one thing I can do wherever I am, whatever time of day it may be. The only way I fail at prayer is to fail to show up. In fact there is a verse that gives us this time frame for prayer: "Pray without ceasing" (1 Thessalonians 5:17 KJV). When it says, "Pray without ceasing," literally, in Greek, "without ceasing" means *without interruption*. Do you know what's funny? When we pray, we always interrupt what we are doing to pause and pray. You say, "Excuse me, we need to pray." Instead of seeing prayer as something that we interrupt our day to do, life is what interrupts my praying without ceasing. Prayer is like internal jogging. Want to stay in shape? Pray without ceasing.

You may be thinking, *How can a busy mother pray constantly?* Well, I know that women think constantly, and those many thoughts can be directed to our heavenly Father and become prayer. Prayer is communication between two people who love each other. Thoughts toward God throughout the day—sharing our concerns about those we love—is praying without ceasing. Prayer is not just about position or posture; it is a reflection of an intimate relationship with the lover of your soul.

Interrupting Life for Prayer

I remember reading an article about Rick Husband, the crew captain of the Columbia Space Shuttle that exploded during re-entry. The article mentioned how Rick loved Jesus and how profound his spiritual walk was. It said that Rick insisted that everyone pause for prayer before any major thing they did as a crew. While I was honestly thrilled about his boldness, I was a little sad when I realized how impressed we are when a Christian "interrupts" life for prayer, when honestly, life interrupts the greatest work we do—which is to pray, because prayer can do what God can do.

As I thought about Rick Husband's leadership, I began to think about a mother's role in her home, and that in reality, she is the crew captain. As the crew captain—"keepers at home" (Titus 2:5 KJV)—she can call for the interruption of life's pace and pray for the crew that she lovingly leads. Before your children blast off for school each day, you can pause and pray for them. You can also pray for them as you are maneuvering the family space shuttle around town—carpooling your kids and their friends.

Why are we so afraid of interrupting life for prayer? I remember one time when I was in college and was driving with another student to visit a needy woman, I said,

"Let's pray before we get there." My friend said, "Well, I will pray since you are driving." And I laughed and said, "I can pray even if I am driving." She said, "How are you going to pray and drive?" I chuckled again. "I pray when I drive all the time!" She was stunned that I pray with my eyes open. Well, if we are going to pray without ceasing, we are going to pray with our eyes open—a lot.

I taught the principle of praying without ceasing, and a young woman, Sami, took it to heart. I was having dinner with this young gal and another friend, and as we were walking out of the restaurant I made the remark, "We'll need to pray about that." Sami said, "Great, let's pray about it right now." So there we were, downtown on a Friday night, right in front of a restaurant with hundreds of people standing around us. This young woman grabbed my hand and I immediately grabbed the other woman's hand. This young, converted Jew just started praying out loud so boldly. As Sami prayed about the need in my life I thought, *Did she have to take the "praying without ceasing" so literally on a Friday night downtown with hundreds of people watching?* And then the Lord really convicted me. *You're ashamed right now, aren't you? You're downtown and people are looking at you all praying and you're ashamed of Me.* So in my mind, I responded, *I'm sorry, Jesus, I'm really not ashamed of you. I really am not.* Nevertheless, there was a moment when I was thinking, *Oh please, don't let anybody walk by and know it's me.*

Women have an advantage in the area of praying without ceasing because of our high verbal capacity. I'm amazed at how seldom women take a chance to pray with their children. I have asked women why they don't pray over their children more regularly. Sometimes the answer is the lack of time; yet many mothers will have time to go to karate practice or dance lessons, but there isn't time for prayer. A mother will brush a child's hair but won't take a moment to pray for the child's heart.

Praying Over Your Children

I tell moms and dads that they should never fear praying over their kids. You can't fail when you pray over your children when they are going to bed. In fact, the only failure in prayer is to *not* pray for your child. When you pray over a child, you can't make a mistake. Your children are not critiquing your prayer—they are listening and learning how to pray. Ask them what they would like you to pray for before they go to sleep. A child's heart is most open when winding down for sleep.

I was so committed to praying with my children that when I'd have a babysitter come over, I'd say, "When Jessie goes down, she doesn't go down without prayer." One time the babysitter exclaimed, "I have to pray over Jessica before she goes to sleep?" I said, "Of course I want you to pray with Jessica, and don't worry, you will be just fine." When our son Ben saw the babysitter's fearful concern about praying over Jessica, he said, "Don't worry, Mom, I'll cover it, I'll pray over Jess when she goes to bed." It is just amazing to me how many people are so uncomfortable with prayer. In our home, praying is like breathing. The four of us are very open verbally, and we are also very open verbally in prayer.

A dear friend told me this story about a time of prayer she had with her little granddaughters. Sandy was babysitting her granddaughters, ages four and two, and it was nap time. The little girls were afraid to go into their room to take a nap. Little Savannah and Libby were telling their grandma that somebody had let them see a scary movie. They told her that when the lights go out they know that monsters will be in their room. So their grandma said, "Do you know what you say the minute you start thinking about the monsters? You say, 'Monsters, Jesus says get out of here!'" So Sandy prayed with Savannah and Libby, and the girls both repeated with their grandmother, "Monsters, Jesus says get out of our room!" They then went off to sleep peacefully for their nap. That night, when their mother got ready to put them to bed, she heard Libby say, "Monsters, Jesus says get out of here!" The mother smiled, knowing that Grandma had prayed with authority over the fear of her children and had instructed the little ones to do likewise.

You may find that story simply amusing, but we really do need to handle our children with that kind of prayer-filled authority. When your kids are afraid, you may be accustomed to saying, "Oh don't worry, we'll look under your beds. There are no witches there. There are no witches in the closet." And while I know that's lovely, and you can talk that little truth pattern out, why not pause and pray instead? When our daughter was little, she had a fear of the dark. Instead of trying to talk Jessica out of her fear, we just prayed over her. Every night we would close the prayer with 2 Timothy 1:7, "For God hath not given us the spirit of fear; but of power, and of love, and of a sound mind" (KJV).

The Praying Chauffeur

The more you pray with your children, the more your children will expect you to pray about the many concerns they tell you. For example, you can stamp the image of a praying mother on their hearts as you drive to school. So often when driving our kids to school, they would be talking about one of the mean teachers at school. I would let them express how mean she was, then I would say, "OK, what do we do with mean teachers?" My kids would reply, "We pray blessings on them." Then I would ask the offended child to express something the teacher may need. "What do you think Mrs. _____ needs?" Immediately our child would say, "She needs to be nicer." Then I would reply, "OK, that's a blessing benefit." Then we would pray for the teacher. Days later my child would share about improvement in the disposition of a mean teacher. We would rejoice in the car on the way home for the obvious answer to prayer. I demonstrated many times through prayer how to overcome evil with good.

This principle also applies to mean teens. Some teenagers are so mean that they eat your child for breakfast emotionally when they first arrive at school. So many moms miss an opportunity to stamp the image of a praying mother in response to something mean that a student did to her teenager. Too often a mom gets hurt about cruel teens and her anger leads her response rather than a prayer-saturated reflex. Praying for the kids who hurt your kids is a noble mission, and those mean young people themselves are a critical mission field.

One more comment for your success as you ink up your stamp of the praying mom: Many moms become exasperated with the demands of carpooling students each week. I have challenged moms to see waiting in line as a chance to pray through their spiral index card prayer lists. I have further challenged moms to consider that the many conversations they overhear are *new prayer assignments.* Chauffeuring kids from one event to another can be a heavenly assignment with a prayerful perspective. Kids seem to be so highly verbal when they are in a car. That is why I always picked my kids up from school whenever I could because so much conversation takes place the moment a child leaves school. I did not want other kids on the bus hearing all the details of the day and then, when my kids come through the door and I asked how the day was, they merely said, "OK." Detail time was drained on the bus and Mom got the crumbs. I wanted the full meal!

Prayer Partners

Do you have a prayer partner? I have no memory of my time as a mother when I didn't have a prayer partner. I was so committed to praying as a mom—even of preschoolers—that a friend and I devised the coolest prayer schedule. Between us, my friend Marguerita and I had five preschoolers. How in the world could we pray with five squealing preschoolers running around? We decided that while they were playing, we would talk and make up our prayer list. When the kids were ready to settle down for a little while, we'd put a video in, and everybody got their Doritos and their Sprite. (I know all health-conscious mothers have just cringed at this terrible treat. For our kids, chips and noncaffeine soda did the trick.) When they were all settled in front of the TV, we would say to them, "OK, we're going in to Marguerita's room and, unless there's blood, don't bang on that door." The kids would all shake their heads, acknowledging our instruction. We'd get in there, get down on our knees, and start praying. The kids rarely knocked on the door, but when they did, we were OK with the interruption, because we would return to our list right after getting someone more to drink or getting someone a favorite blanket. Years later, I have pondered the legacy that Marguerita and I gave our children as we went into her room and prayed while they were chomping on Doritos and watching their favorite video.

So many mothers of preschoolers arrange play dates. I would like to suggest that during these play dates, moms can have prayer dates. You can make your lists and even start praying as you watch your children sliding down the slide. Mothers sit together and talk and watch their kids play all the time. Why not watch your kids play while you pray? Make a list; it will help keep you on track, even when little Jessi falls and you have to pause and brush the dirt off her hands! After kissing the boo-boo, you can return to talking to Abba.

At this time in my life, my prayer partner does not live nearby. So once a week on Wednesday mornings, we call each other. Before we call each other, we record our individual prayer requests in our prayer journal. When we call each other, we share our requests and then we pray over the phone. We have a record of all that God has done through our prayer partnership, and the miracles that we have seen in answer to our prayers would rock your world! Our prayer partnership is framed by the fabulous passage in Matthew 18:

"Again, I tell you that if two of you on earth agree [harmonize] about anything you ask for, it will be done for you by my Father in heaven." (Matthew 18:19)

I cannot sing, but I have been harmonizing in prayer for almost three decades as a wife and mother. If you don't have a prayer partner, ask Jesus to show you today someone you can harmonize with in prayer.

One time, my prayer partner was at a conference with me and she wanted to pray over me before I spoke. As I was going to the bathroom one more time before putting on my microphone, who came running behind me? My precious prayer partner! We stood right there in the bathroom and prayed. Several women from the conference remarked to us later that they were afraid to flush the toilet when they heard us praying. I assured them that my prayer partner and I have been praying without ceasing and without regard for location—bathrooms, cars, beach, phones, and so on for years now. C. W. Gaddy said, "The meaning of prayer is not determined by proper mechanics, but by personal authenticity."

Where can you pray? Anywhere:
• Pray in prison. (Acts 16:25)
• Pray by a river. (Acts 16:13)
• Pray on the beach in beach chairs.
• Pray walking on railroad tracks.
• Pray in the car with your best friend, your kids, or others.
• Pray at sporting events.
• Pray at the gym—go through cards on the elliptical, stepper, or bike.
• Pray while waiting in the doctor's office.

What do you need to pray with another mother for all of your children? Think of your sessions together as choir rehearsals, and the Holy Spirit is your chorus director. You need your duet's music folder (prayer journal). Enter requests, and enter praises, and use your journal to stay on the same page. Write down your requests before getting together or dialing—then share requests. Rehearse God's goodness; anticipate answers to prayer. Don't forget to say "thank You." Make your requests—one by one …with Holy Spirit directions (additions).

Prayer Roll-a-dex

This section is probably the most important aspect of praying without ceasing as a mom. As a mother who wanted to pray faithfully, I often struggled with concentrating and remembering so many requests. God showed me a surefire way of staying on task and not getting sidetracked. I purchased two things: a package of 4 x 6 index cards and a 4 x 6 photo album. I wrote out several categories to place my prayer requests under, and each card became a holy reminder. I put the prayer cards in a photo album to keep them in good shape. When I first started this method, I carried the 4 x 6 cards in my purse with a rubber band holding them together. The wear and tear on the cards motivated me to buy the photo album to keep the cards in great shape and to go through them more easily. Here are some of my categories, which are just suggestions. They are not exhaustive; you will probably think of others.

Jackie's Prayer Cards—Holy Reminders
1. People who need Jesus (whom I know personally)
2. Married couples (glorify God)
3. Young singles (wait for God's best—Bozo vs. Boaz)

4. Youth (God Squad or Blazing Torches)
5. Missionaries
6. Spiritual leaders (pastors, Bible teachers)
7. Family members
8. Friends
9. Terminally ill
10. Emotionally ill (need healing of heart wounds)
11. My heart dreams and desires
12. Individual cards for my husband and each child
13. Christian professional athletes and their wives (their influence for Christ)
14. Christian celebrities

As Paul wrote to Timothy, "I urge, then, first of all, that requests, prayers, intercession and thanksgiving be made for everyone" (1 Timothy 2:1). Here is a recent letter from a woman who heard about the Stamp of a Praying Woman:

> The *pray without ceasing* talk you did—what an awesome concept! I stole your idea about making a prayer book out of a spiral index card book. I am not up to the "interrupt prayer with life" level but that is my goal (1 Thessalonians 5:17). Well, I carried the "theft" a step further. I work part-time in a Christian school, and the art teacher was hunting for ideas for Mother's Day. I shared with him my thoughts about the spiral index card prayer book. He found spiral-bound note cards for 50 cents each and the students were thrilled with the idea! So now, we have at least 60 mothers getting ready to receive a Jackie Kendall–inspired Mother's Day gift.

What should a woman do with her prayer roll-a-dex? Carry it with you—in your purse, in your car. Women are always waiting somewhere. In order to have a nice attitude during prolonged waiting, I always have my prayer cards with me. Whether I am at a doctor's office, getting my hair done, waiting at the airport for my husband to return home, or on a long plane flight, I can always pray. I do it on the elliptical machine at the gym. There I am, exercising and flipping through my cards, and I even manage not to break my neck! As I go through the photo album, everybody thinks I'm admiring pictures of my kids or grandkids. Some ask me if the cards are for a course I am taking in college.

One more aspect of prayer that I want to encourage you about is long-term repetition. It is so easy to grow weary of praying for a long time and not see results. God knew that this might happen, so He gave us a great pep-talk verse for praying without seeing immediate results. "Let us not become weary in doing good, for at the proper time we will reap a harvest if we do not give up" (Galatians 6:9). In that verse the word *weary* means fainthearted and exasperated. I have people on my prayer cards whom I have prayed over for years. For some I have seen great miracles, and for others I have had to resist growing fainthearted in not yet seeing answers. In the last seven months, I have seen more answers to prayer than I have in years. I think I am in the "proper time." This season comes after years of praying for the same people.

The Holy Point

Have you ever found yourself speechless in prayer—whether it was because of agony or aggravation? Have you ever been so burdened for someone that you had no idea how to even begin praying for the person? Well, I have found myself speechless in agony and aggravation, and the Lord has given me a creative idea called *the holy point*. He gave me this idea after I read this quote about the power of prayer:

> This power is so rich and so mobile that all we have to do when we pray is to point to the persons or things to which we desire to have this power applied, and He, the Lord of this power, will direct the necessary power to the desired person or thing. (*Prayer*, by O. Hallesby)

Now whenever I am burdened (or aggravated), I simply take my right hand and point in the direction of the person I am concerned about. Then I lift my eyes toward heaven as I point, and I release this person, *again*, into God's capable hands. I am now pointing—north, south, east, and west—from my kitchen, at the gym, on my bed in the middle of the night. This *holy point* method has helped me to keep from being a frustrated intercessor, since as I point and look for a moment at heaven, I am reminded again of the One who is in charge.

> God's love is meteoric, his loyalty astronomic, his purpose titanic, his verdicts oceanic. Yet in his largeness nothing gets lost; not a man, not a mouse, slips through the cracks. How exquisite your love, O God! (Psalm 36:5–7 The Message)

The other day at the gym, an unsaved woman came in. I shared with her previously and she began avoiding me. Since I couldn't talk to her, I began praying for her.

Without her knowing, I pointed at her and asked Jesus to open her eyes. After I pointed in her direction, a joy began to flood my soul. I released her to the only One who can open her eyes. I will be pointing south many times during the month of July, as my precious husband and daughter are serving in southern locations. Whenever I begin to be anxious, the holy point south and the glance upward will restore God's peace. This holy point is the only time we can live outside the courtesy rule: "It isn't polite to point."

Application: The Stamp of the Praying Mom

A Tender Prayer by a Walking Christmas Tree

Two weeks ago Jessica said, "Mom, come see what Ben wants to wear to church tonight." Ben had on an olive T-shirt, olive corduroy baggy shorts, *red wool socks,* and Adidas sandals—he looked like a Christmas tree. I laughed and told Ben it was original and that is what I liked about him. Yes, we let Ben go to Sunday night service dressed in the above, and what a shock when the pastor asked at the close of the evening service, "Where is Ben Kendall?" Ben raised his hand and the pastor asked him to come up on the platform and close the service in prayer. When Ben got to the podium, the pastor noticed his socks and said, "Nice socks, Ben!" Youth closing our service was not a regular event (in fact, no one can remember such an event in years). Ben was excited about the privilege of praying in front of the whole church and he felt a special closeness with our pastor. People were impressed with not only Ben's bright red socks but also his tender prayer. Teens are such a blessing because they break up the monotony that life seems to produce for middle-aged adults.

Surfing and Intercession

You may be wondering how in the world I have linked surfing with intercession, but they have been linked in our family by our son. Let me explain. We live near the beach. The other day after checking out the surf—it looked like Lake Atlantic—Ben was so disappointed. After a week of not being able to surf, we did not have a happy camper in our car. As we were driving home, Ben said, "Can we pray for some good surf?" I was ready to say yes when Jessica responded, "No way! I am not praying for big waves!" Then Ben replied, "Well, then at least be reverent when I pray for some waves." I wanted to laugh, but I worked hard to keep a straight face. Ben began to pray for good waves, then he started to pray about his attitude and being content with "Lake Atlantic," then he proceeded to pray for one of the parents in the youth group who was having heart problems, then for a friend who had "spiritual heart problems," then he moved to the needs of the whole youth group, then he prayed for my speaking engagements, and he went on and on. When he was finished he said, "Excuse me, you guys; when I started praying, it felt like something exploded inside

my heart and I couldn't stop praying." We assured Ben
that he never has to apologize for lengthy intercession.

A Major God Talk on the Deck

Jessica and seven of her closest friends (guys and girls)
were invited to go away to Lake Placid, Florida, with
a wonderful family. The first night, while the teenagers
were sitting out on the dock looking up at the stars,
a serious "God talk" began, and the teenagers talked until
3:00 A.M. about all their questions and doubts. They came
to the conclusion after listening to one another that their
doubts could only be handled by a stronger faith in God.
On Sunday morning the teens were asked to share, and
I was told later what Jessica had said and the tears that
her comments provoked. One of the remarks Jessica
made was, "As the summer continues and we don't
always see one another, you can be sure that I will be
talking about each of you, talking about you to the
Father." She had also read an excerpt from *My Utmost for
His Highest* and Philippians 1:3-11. God is doing such
a sweet and welcome work among Jessica and her
friends. The Tuesday night girls' Bible study in our home
grew out of this fresh move of God in our midst.

Qualification: Faithfulness

Sometimes as a wife, I could very easily be like Mrs. Job,
who discouraged her husband and tried to point him
away from following God (see Job 2:9). For example, this
summer, when Ken was preparing for a big WAY-FM mission trip, I had access to information about the trip that
began to stack up as one of the "harder trips" Ken would

lead. Although I was praying and even fasting about the trip, several times as a junior Mrs. Job I wanted to say, "Ken, why don't you do some other form of full-time Christian service?" Of course, I kept my thoughts between God and me. God had been showing me in Ezra and Nehemiah that *anyone* building for God can count on the enemy's presence and attacks. Well, good old faithful Ken packed his duffel bag and set out on another mission trip for Jesus.

Unknown to Ken or me, someone on this particular trip was closely observing Ken's servant leadership and the format of a World Servants mission trip. Holly was so touched by the incredible work and ministry accomplished on the trip that eight weeks later she wrote a letter to Ken at the World Servants office. With the note came a letter that said, "It is our pleasure to inform you that the Board of Directors of the GHC Foundation has approved a grant to World Servants Inc. in the amount of $40,000 for community leadership training." The gift to World Servants was perfectly timed. The next day Ken called to thank Holly and ask why the gift was from the foundation in the name of a boy named Peter. Holly then told the story of the death of their son Peter, whom they knew would have made a difference in the world. So in his name they have a foundation that gives gifts to organizations that are making a difference in the world.

That gift left everyone at World Servants pretty overwhelmed with God's goodness. However, no one was as blown away as this Mrs. Job. Here I was fussing and whining inside my head, while Abba was grinning in pleasure at the faithfulness of one of His boys even in a very hard place. Abba knew the gift that was coming to remind this Mrs. Job that the most important qualification for serving in the harvest is faithfulness.

How Long Do You Pray?

Thirteen years ago, I went to dinner with a woman and shared Jesus with her. She listened, but she was not ready to surrender to Him. I had met her through my mother's work. Recently she called me from Boston; she wanted me to know that she had given her heart to Jesus, and now she wants to share the good news with others—just like I did in that restaurant 13 years ago. Her phone call reminded me to not grow weary in well doing—we will reap a blessing from God for what we sow, but the timing is not predictable.

Prayer for Our Timid Child

Our Jessica used to be painfully shy. When she was little, after reading to her each night, we would pray over her and we would close the prayer each night quoting "For God has not given us a spirit of fear, but of power and of love and of a sound mind" (2 Timothy 1:7 NKJV).

Last Sunday we went to hear Jessica and the school choir sing. She was asked to speak before she did her solo. Jessica began her testimony quoting the above verse. She told the story of how her parents prayed this Scripture over her as a shy, fearful child and how they continue to pray about her spirit of fear. She shared how she is learning to choose faith over fear on a daily basis. What an invaluable privilege to pray over our children every night. Jessica as a 17-year-old will come and tell us that she is going to bed—which is always our cue to come and pray over her.

Kendall Last Supper

During the last year, a joke with our kids is, "Mom is treating every supper together like the Last Supper!" I admit that I have sensed that major changes are coming and I wanted to give extra attention to the meals our family had together. Well, three weeks ago on a Thursday night, Ben said, "I guess tonight is going to be a Last Supper together for a while." Ben was moving to Jacksonville the next day for a three-month internship. I had made a very special dinner and Ken had found a reading he wanted to share. The reading was on hope, and it closed with these words: "Hope is not a granted wish or a favor performed; no, it is far greater than that. It is a zany, unpredictable dependence on a God who loves to surprise us out of our socks and be there in the flesh to see our reaction" (*God Came Near*, by Max Lucado).

When Ken finished reading Max Lucado's remarks on hope, he suggested that we lay hands on Ben and pray God's blessing on his time in Jacksonville. As each of us prayed, the tears poured. Later that night as Ken and I were talking, I told him how much I appreciated the reading he chose and our prayer time. Ken said, "I didn't know it was going to hurt this much"—and he began to weep again. We had a duet of tears late into the night, as we reminisced about 20 years loving our Benny.

We are adjusting to Ben being gone, and our comfort is that this opportunity is such a gift from God that we can only rejoice when Ben calls and he is so excited about all he is learning. A verse that reflects our hearts today is Isaiah 26:12:"LORD, you will grant us peace, for all we have accomplished is really from you" (NLT).

Ben and I moved his "stuff" up to Jacksonville to a friend's guesthouse, and I told him how his daddy had begun crying again at bedtime. Ben said, "I understand his tears. He is losing his best friend, Mom, apart from you." Ken has always said his only hobby is his family and he and Ben have been on quite an adventure together for two decades.

Big Brother to the Rescue

During Jessica's first week in college, she not only got physically sick with horrible allergies, but she was also very homesick. Her brother called her all pumped because he had come from a Bible study. When he heard how discouraged Jessica sounded, he tried to give her an inspiring pep talk. Then he decided it would be better to pray for her. Later Ben told me, "Mom, I started to pray for her and I could tell the prayer wasn't helping. Then I remembered a time when I was living in Jacksonville and I was lonely and discouraged—suddenly I began to cry in compassion for Jessica and then the most awesome prayer just poured from my heart." After Ben prayed for Jessica, she was sitting on her bed reading her Bible when two girls knocked on her door and asked her what she was doing. When she told them she was reading her Bible, they asked, "Do you really like to do that?" Jessica's immediate remark: "I can't imagine a day without reading my Bible." She is now praying for those girls!

The Kendall Comfort Connection

Recently a precious friend of ours lost her beloved grandfather suddenly to acute leukemia. The night he died, she called from the hospital and asked if she could come to our home. The four of us were home, and we had the privilege of loving on this grieving young woman. We cried with her, laughed with her, prayed with her, hugged her, and stroked her hair. She said through tears, "I knew this was the perfect place to come." Ben immediately responded, "We Kendalls are unfortunately experts in the area of the grief process." As I watched Ken, Ben, and Jessica love on this grieving friend, I reflected on all the deaths that groomed us to be *The Kendall Comfort Connection*. Jessica said, "Now I know why I came home this weekend—it was to be here for Courtney in this time of such great loss." The God of All Comfort used us that night and again at the funeral. What a privilege to weep with those who weep.

An Early Mother's Day Gift

"O LORD my God, you have done many miracles for us. Your plans for us are too numerous to list. If I tried to recite all your wonderful deeds, I would never come to the end of them" (Psalm 40:5 NLT). I have had so many wonderful answers to prayer in relation to Ben and Jessica that I find myself looking down at my feet to make sure I haven't floated off the ground. This little space does not permit the retelling of all God's wonderful deeds in Ben's and Jessica's lives. Several times during the last couple weeks, Ben has called so excited about something he has learned at the Bible study he is attending each Wednesday morning. God has blessed Ben with some very solid young men who have taken him under their wings as he learns to soar again with Jesus. Whenever I get off the phone with Ben, all I can think is that there is no greater joy than to see my children walk in truth (3 John 4). Then the phone rings again and Jessica is talking about a summer internship that she has been chosen for. She will work with senior high students. An absolute bonus is that she will be working in West Palm Beach at First Baptist Church. We'll have another summer with Jessica at home, where we can cheer her on as she grows more in love with Jesus.

Questions:
For Individual Reflection
or Group Study

1. How would you define prayer? (Matthew 6:5-15)
2. What keeps you from praying without ceasing? (1 Thessalonians 5:17; 1 Timothy 2:1-3)
3. Do you have a prayer roll-a-dex? What would hinder you from getting one this week? (Matthew 6:5-6)
4. Share one of your greatest answers to prayer.
5. Do you have a prayer partner? (Matthew 18:19-20) Prayer is often better as a duet; review the section in this chapter about prayer partners.
6. Do you see the challenges in your children's lives as prayer assignments? (Philippians 4:6-7; Psalm 119:147; Ephesians 6:18; Hebrews 4:16)

Chapter 4

STAMP THE IMAGE OF
Loving God's Word

**Principle:
Love for God's Word
can be contagious.**

G et your inkpad ready; here is another stamp. This stamp was actually given to all parents thousands of years ago.

Love the LORD your God with all your heart and with all your soul and with all your strength. These commandments that I give you today are to be upon your hearts. *Impress* them on your children. *Talk* about them when you *sit* at home and when you *walk* along the road, when you *lie down* and when you *get up*. Tie them as symbols on your hands and bind them on your foreheads. Write them on the doorframes of your houses and on your gates. (Deuteronomy 6:5–9, italics added)

What is this ancient stamp? It is the stamp of a student of the Word of God. Being a student in the Word is another name for being a perpetual learner. As a constantly enrolled student of the Word, you can teach your children with confidence throughout the day about the hope that is in God's Word. Saint Augustine said, "God's Word is shallow enough to not drown the young, but deep enough that the greatest theologian will never touch the bottom."

Ben discovered this truth one day. After an argument between him and Jessica, when they had worked things out verbally (which included asking forgiveness and praying), Ben still seemed disturbed. I asked him if something was wrong and he said, "I don't understand how I could have great devotions this morning and then argue in the car with Jessica." I told him that having devotions does not keep a person from sinning, but having devotions helps one respond properly when one has sinned (asking his sister's forgiveness). "I've banked your promises in the vault of my heart so I won't sin myself bankrupt" (Psalm 119:11 The Message).

Have You Spent Time at Jesus's Feet?

Do your children know that every day you attend school "at the feet of Jesus" (Luke 10:38–42)? Do your children know where in your home you have your "quiet time spot" where you meet with Jesus? Do your children know where you keep your Bible and journal? Years ago when I was in college, I took a class from a woman who was the mother of seven kids. She talked about her "special place," and I would imagine she was talking about a place where she could escape her kids. She told the class that her special place was a chair where her Bible and her journal and a pen were always in place, ready for the perpetual learner to return. It was always a little pile, but it was her pile ready for time with God. This mother didn't have a separate room or a mountaintop—she had a "quiet time chair."

When our children were preschoolers, wherever I was, they would find me. Even in my special chair, they found me. So how did I adapt to their presence when I wanted to concentrate on God's presence in His Word and prayer? Here is what I did. (I am ADHD and it worked in spite of the apparent chaos.) I put all of their junk—toys, blocks, books, etc.—in a large plastic clothesbasket and placed it by my special chair. They would start playing, and I would start reading. The moment they started climbing on me or asking me a question, the *first* thing I did was place my finger firmly on the verse that I was reading. After I had marked the verse with my finger, I asked, "What do you need, sweetheart?" Often a few seconds of attention was all they really needed. Then I would say, "Play nicely, because momma is trying to read her Bible." Many times my children would go get a book and try to imitate my concentration when I was reading. Today they are both students of God's Word, and I know that modeling began when they were barely crawling and walking.

You may think such a method is a waste of time. You may think that a mother couldn't possibly get something out of God's Word in the swirl of such chaos. Well, for some that may be true, yet I watch mothers do *all kinds* of activities with their kids around—reading magazines, talking on the phone, watching television, doing schoolwork—so how can we say we can't read God's Word with kids around? When I was trying to concentrate and get through my quiet time while my children were climbing all over me, interrupting me, spilling stuff on me, God not only understood but He was honored by my valiant efforts.

In the middle of the night when I would get up to feed one of my children, I'd always have those little lights that go over one's shoulders on the bed and I'd sit there and read my Bible and feed my babies. Of course, since I was up in the middle of the night, I was exhausted all day. And that's when I found a special verse in 2 Samuel 24. David was being offered some animals for free in order to offer a sacrifice. But David replied, "No, I insist on paying you for it. I will not sacrifice to the Lord my God burnt offerings that cost me nothing" (2 Samuel 24:24). I thought about that verse. *Don't offer that which costs you nothing.* Then I realized, *This is costing me. I'm trying to concentrate and feed my baby. I'm doing what has to be done at this phase in my life. I'm still seeking God even when it's costing me some sleep time.* The Holy One knows you are a mother. He knows the context of your life. He understands what it's costing you.

To those who feel too busy to be in the Word, I always say, "A Bible that's falling apart reflects a life that isn't." So be careful. Don't let your children or life circumstances sabotage your time with God each day.

Did You Get Your Seven?

Why is a daily time in God's Word so important for a mom? How much time is a breathlessly busy mom supposed to spend in God's Word? I have been challenging moms for years to at least *get her seven minutes with God.* When I was a brand-new Christian, I knew nothing about the Word of God. I did not know one verse when I asked Jesus to come into my heart on April 15, 1967. When the Youth for Christ leader gave me my first Bible, the only thing he asked me to do was to read my Bible for *seven minutes.* This youth leader knew that as a new Christian, if I read more than seven I would probably get too confused. I began to meet other young people who were given the same challenge to get their *seven minutes* with God daily. Even if you work full-time and have a busy family, you have time for seven minutes with God. Whether I'm teaching student conferences or talking to professional athletes, I challenge people to get seven minutes in the Word daily. Do you know how many seven-minute increments we've got in a day? Every day you have 205 chances for seven minutes with God.

Since 1988, I have used the One Year Bible format. So many people get bogged down trying to read through the Bible. The One Year Bible splits your daily reading into four simple parts. Each day includes one section of the Old Testament, one section of the New Testament, a reading from the book of Psalms, and a verse or two from the book of Proverbs—an easy format and four chances to get something during your short time in God's Word.

The first two women who mentored me as a new Christian gave the same life challenge. These women never met each other, but they both challenged me to be a woman of the Word. A common phrase used by my first mentor, Mamie Hinch, was "Child, what does the Word say?" My second mentor, M. E. Cravens, came along in college and tattooed my heart with this statement, "There is no success, no happiness, and no fulfillment in life apart from a consistent, daily growing relationship with Jesus through the Word."

M. E. Cravens laid a foundation for such confidence in God's Word that a sign was posted in my heart: *Despair— No Trespassing Here.* How did she build such confidence? The first mentoring homework she gave me was an instruction to get a red pen and read through the book of Psalms, circling the word *trust* wherever I found it. This project gave birth to a faith that has not failed though I have walked several times through the valley of the shadow of death (the suicides of two of my siblings and my own recovery from the wounds of sexual abuse, to mention a few).

I am constantly challenging young people to get this "holy habit" established in their lives *now*. If you don't get this thing going when you're young, it is so hard later. That's why I'm traveling and telling young kids, "Get this habit down good." So many teens have the smoking habit, the premarital sex habit, the drug habit, the shopping habit, the dieting habit. They get all these habits established as young teens. It only takes 28 days of consistent activity to form a habit. How great it would be if more of our teens got into the holy habit of reading the Bible each day! It should be part of everyone's daily agenda.

My mentor Bettye Galbraith has repeatedly said, "The absence of God's Word in your life robs your faith in God's ability." Bettye is the smartest grandmother I know. Every week she drives over to her daughter's house and listens to her grandsons (sixth and eighth grade) recite the verses they have memorized for their Bible class. Bettye is passionate about getting young people into the Word. She knows the fallacy of passing school but flunking life because one does not know the great wisdom that is found in God's Word.

One last comment about establishing this holy habit: If you miss a day or two, don't let the enemy detour you into such discouragement that a day or two turns into a month or two. If you missed yesterday, today is a new day, and there are 205 more opportunities for you to *get your seven!*

Do You Know the God of the Bible?

How can someone know the Word but not know God? This mystery is the difference of

Knowledge vs. Intimacy

Rituals vs. Relationship

Religion vs. Christianity

Scripture itself says it is possible to know the Bible and not know God: "They didn't recognize Him or realize that He is the One the prophets had written about *though they hear the prophets' words read every Sabbath*" (Acts 13:27 NLT, italics added).

Parade Magazine once carried a story about a little village church in Kalinovka, Russia, where attendance at Sunday school picked up after the minister started handing out candy to the peasant children. One of the most faithful was a pug-nosed, pugnacious lad who recited his Scriptures with proper devotion, pocketed his reward, and then fled to the fields to munch on it. The minister took a liking to the boy and persuaded him to attend church school. The boy preferred doing this to household chores, so he went. By offering other rewards, the teacher managed to teach the boy *all the verses* of four Gospels. He won a special prize for learning all of Matthew, Mark, Luke, and John by heart and reciting them nonstop in a church service. Sixty years later, he still liked to recite Scriptures, but in a context that would horrify his old teacher. You see, the prize pupil, who memorized so much of the Bible, was Nikita Khrushchev, the late communist Czar.

People can spend their lives learning the Word without ever knowing God intimately. That last paragraph was also a reminder of the many ways a person can "use" the Word for his or her own agenda. If a communist czar can use the Word to make his points, I shouldn't be surprised when I see a person using God's Word to bully and manipulate other believers. Beware of the Khrushchev spirit among us. "Your enemy the devil prowls around like a roaring lion looking for someone to devour" (1 Peter 5:8).

A Death Grip on the Word

I just finished reading Carol Kent's newest book, *When I Lay My Isaac Down*. I could not put it down. I cried and prayed the whole time I was reading it. This book encouraged me to have unshakable faith in unthinkable circumstances. I found a Scripture that gives us a glimpse of the means of such unshakable faith. "But the seed on good soil stands for those with a noble and good heart, who hear the word, *retain* it, and by *persevering* produce a crop" (Luke 8:15, italics added).

That verse is from one of Jesus's most familiar parables: the sower and the seed. But the Lord showed me something new in a familiar place. Why is one person fruitful in response to God's Word while another is fruitless? In this parable, what makes this particular person fruitful— capable of producing a crop? Two words hold the key. The first word I looked up was *retain* (Greek, *katecho*), which means to "maintain possession of firmly, like a death grip." The second word was *persevering* (Greek, *hypomone*), which means "doesn't cave in during trials but endures."

Now what did this person have a "death grip" on? Simple answer: the Word. Those "who hear the *word, retain it.*"

By keeping a "death grip" on God's Word, a person will not cave in during trials. Every day when I spend time in God's Word, I am checking my grip, making sure all ten of my fingers are wrapped tightly around the hope of God's Word. I can't retain unless I maintain a consistent grip on the Word. Have you checked your grip lately? Are you caving in under stressful circumstances? Have you released your grip on God's Word? When I loosen my grip on God's Word, I schedule my own avalanche—a landslide cave-in on my soul. This landslide prevents the growth of a crop for God's glory.

In the book *When I Lay My Isaac Down,* Carol Kent describes her "death grip" on her hope in Jesus. Every day she is facing unimaginable suffering and yet her faith is not caving in but *enduring*—unshakable. As sorrows increase around us, we cannot afford to miss our daily grip on God's Word. With a "death grip" on God's Word, we will be fruitful no matter what our circumstances—even if they are unthinkable.

Application: The Stamp of a Student of God's Word

Deuteronomy on Sanibel Island

During our family vacation on Sanibel Island, we bought a journal and titled it "Kendall Vacation Memories." For a couple of days, we recounted memories of our family vacations. We started with our first trip to Sanibel Island in 1985. It was so neat recording the different incidents that were stored in Ben and Jessica's memories…dolphins in the shallow waters; starfish, sand dollars, and crabs; bike riding to Jerry's market; Ben getting six stitches in his head; the midnight turtle patrol; the surprise visit from California friends. The kids rambled on and on, and I wrote until I had writer's cramp. This journal will travel with us on our family trips so we can record new memories and cherish old ones.

While on Sanibel Island this year, we sailed to Cayo Costa Island. As we approached the island, we sailed into what seemed like a dolphin sanctuary. Our little boat was surrounded by a half-dozen dolphins. Squealing with excitement, we photographed these graceful creatures. As I reflected on our special moments with the dolphins, I could not help but think of Romans 1:20. "For since the creation of the world God's invisible qualities—his eternal power and divine nature—have been clearly seen, being understood from what has been made, so that men are without excuse."

We are so grateful for a God who not only paints Himself in sunsets, on the ocean deep, on mountains high, and among the redwoods, but also imprints Himself on people near and far (Deuteronomy 6:4-9). Our record of good memories is but a small mirror of the Word's record of God's goodness.

Mom's Got a New Necklace

Recently, while Ken was out of town, Ben and I were having devotions together and he remarked about a verse that he found in Matthew. I asked him when he was reading the book of Matthew, and he said, "Oh, I've been setting my alarm to wake up 15 minutes earlier so I can read my Bible."

Of course, my response was deep: "Really!"

Then I told Ben what Proverbs says about the joy that a wise son brings his father and mother. I shared with him how several times in the book of Proverbs we are encouraged to keep the truth as close to us as a necklace around one's neck (Proverbs 3:3). I told Ben that his wise behavior was like a beautiful necklace around my neck. When I prayed with Ben, my heart was full of praise for the work God was doing in Ben's private devotional world. I kissed him goodnight, and as he walked toward the bathroom he said, "Mom, I love you, and I sure hope you like your new necklace." I confess I was overwhelmed.

Devotional Pull Chain

Ben expressed his concern about being inconsistent in relation to his devotions since school is out for the summer and his morning schedule is not consistent. So he created a reminder by hanging a sign from his fan's pull chain. The sign said in capital letters: DEVOTIONS.

He was excited to show us his "devotional reminder." What a rebuke and challenge to all of us! What a blessing to be driving through upstate New York and to glance into the rearview mirror and see Ben reading his Bible and writing in his journal. "Blessed is the man who finds wisdom, the man who gains understanding, for she is more profitable than silver and yields better returns than gold" (Proverbs 3:13–14). May we all invest time in wisdom, which has a better return than even Wal-Mart stock.

A Cheerleader for Kings and the King

Jessica and I were reading a teen devotional that we had given her for Christmas, and when I read the verse for the day Jessica said, "Hey, that is the verse I have in my locker." I asked her to tell me more about this verse in her locker. She said, "I really like the verse so I wrote it on a 3-by-5-inch card and taped it to the inside of my locker." The verse she chose was: "I planted the seed, Apollos watered it, but God made it grow" (1 Corinthians 3:6). I asked her why she chose that particular verse and she said, "Each person has a different job to do for God."

Her remark touched my heart. Jessica already has a strong sense of the significance of being Jessica and not any other person when cheering for Jesus. Last week when she was experiencing fear about a situation, I suggested that she find a verse on "fear" and put it in her locker. She chose four verses, two for her mirror and two for her locker. She was so excited when the verse for the day on her favorite Christian radio station was a verse she had chosen for her mirror.

Jessica is about to win a trophy for being the most spirited cheerleader. We have successfully kept this honor secret from her. The cheerleaders voted for the girl on their squad who was the most enthusiastic and positive during practice as well as the games. We are thrilled for Jessica, and we are pleased that she has worked so hard as a cheerleader for Kings Academy. We are even more thrilled about her growing boldness in cheering spiritually for her King.

Major League Ballplayer

When the baseball strike ended, it brought the ballplayers to West Palm Beach for three weeks. After an evening with a ballplayer and his wife, during which we talked about the Lord for hours, Ben said, "I need to be alone." When I went to check on him later, I found him reading his Bible. He looked up and said, "After being around John and Michele Wetteland, all I wanted to do is go and read my Bible." Ben's remark caused me to reflect back three years ago when he had begun his own personal journey of daily reading his Bible. I realized he made that decision in April, and that was the same time that we had spent several evenings at our dining room table with this same ballplayer and his wife talking with passion and enthusiasm about the Word of God. Of course, I realized that God laid the foundation for Ben's spiritual journey through ten years of nightly devotions with his dad (sometimes Mom), but I also realize the powerful influence of a young couple so radically committed to God and His Word. That night when I went to bed, I prayed that I would so walk with Jesus that when people have spent time with me, they would end up thirsty for more of Jesus.

Love Letter Taken for Granted

Before Ken goes out of town, he always goes to the store and purchases cards for us. The night before he leaves, after he has finished packing, he writes each of us an encouraging letter. He usually mails the cards at the airport and, in a couple of days, his love letters arrive. He has done this for years. In fact, my mom thinks he is the president of the Send-a-Card Club!

During his recent trip to Guatemala, my two cards from Ken arrived the second day he was gone and the cards for Ben and Jessica arrived the third day. I placed Ben and Jessica's cards at their places at the dinner table. When Ben got home from school, I told him he had a card from his dad. Ben's response, "Cool." He started his Spanish homework, and the card remained sealed and unread. After he finished his homework, he turned on his favorite surfing program. When he sat down at the table to eat dinner, he picked the card up and finally read the loving note from his dad. As I saw him reading the note, I was disappointed that he hadn't seemed anxious to read the love from his dad. As my heart ached about Ben's response, the Lord said, "Jackie, his attitude is like many of My children, who daily take My love and faithfulness for granted." Ben has always had a loving and faithful father, and he is used to Ken's consistent love and affection. Sometimes we take for granted the goodness of a loved one. I was blown away by the reality of a father's love letter taken for granted. Having been raised by an abusive father, I cannot comprehend even one loving card from my father—much less hundreds, which our children have received over the last 16 years.

This incident convicted me of the way I so easily take God's love letter for granted. Just as homework and TV distracted Ben from his father's loving card, so many things daily distract me from quality time reading the love letter from my heavenly Father. Ken's cards to us reveal such care in the card chosen and the message written. Every time I read the Word of God, the message is personal and appropriate for my needs. Hallmark can't compete with God's love letter to His children.

Motivated by God, Not M&M

Our youth pastor asked Ben if he would be willing to speak briefly to the youth group on Wednesday night. When Ben told us about this opportunity, I began to pray that his motivation would not be M&M (men and mom). It is so easy to do things to please one's parents or one's youth pastor. I was concerned that Ben would know that his assignment was from God. So I began to pray that God would give Ben a specific message that was clearly provoked by God's Spirit and not M&M.

Ben came home from school excited the day he was scheduled to speak. He said, "Mom, I know what God wants me to share with the teens tonight. He wants me to talk about obeying God not because of fear, but because of love. I am going to share that the more I read my Bible, the more I fall in love with Jesus." Ben was having a hard time spiritually last year. Now he is sharing with his peers about a clearer understanding of God's love because of the choice he has made to spend time daily with Jesus. Here is the quote Ben decided to use: "If God had a refrigerator, your picture would be on it. If He had a wallet, your photo would be in it. Face it, friend. He's crazy about you."

Miss Fanny's Hat

Two weeks ago, I had the privilege of reading to two of my favorite little people, Mahala and Harry, before they went to sleep. As I was reading one of their favorites, we came to the end of the story and I began to cry. The children were concerned and I told them that I miss the privilege of reading to my own children. Mahala said, "Hey, I have another book you can read."

One day when our children were preschoolers, I began to calculate how many books I had read to our children during one year and I figured it had to be about 1,460—reading a couple of books before nap time and at nighttime every day. The other day while clearing a storage area in Jessica's closet, I came upon all the books that were our kids' favorites. I decided to store these books in a treasure box and mark the box, "Treasures for Our Grandchildren." If Jesus tarries, I am already looking forward to having grandchildren on my lap, resting between my shoulders...listening to their parent's favorite books. Reading allows a time of bonding that makes me think of the tender expression in Deuteronomy 33:12, "Let the beloved of the LORD rest secure in him, for he shields him all day long, and the one the LORD loves *rests between his shoulders*" (italics mine).

Ken and I have made several mistakes as parents, but one thing we feel good about is the choice to not allow anyone or anything to keep us from reading to our children. Even when we had guests in our home, Ken and I would excuse ourselves and go read God's Word to our children before they went to sleep. Reading provided a perfect bridge for prayer time with our children, which continues to this day.

She's Ready to Go

One morning I was sitting on my bed reading my Bible and writing in my journal. The phone rang, and as I ran for the phone, Jessica also came running for the phone. The call was for her, and as she walked toward her room, I noticed that her Bible and journal were open on the bed. When I thought about each of us in our own rooms reading our Bibles, I smiled walking back to my room and this thought came to me: *She is ready to leave us and go to college because she has the "holy habit" in its proper place.*

A couple of nights later, she and I were up talking until 1:30 A.M. She was sharing a particular ministry opportunity that she was a little nervous about, and when she confessed her fear to God, that very morning in her devotions He gave her this verse: "Be strong and courageous, and do the work. Do not be afraid or discouraged, for the LORD God, my God, is with you. He will not fail you or forsake you until all the work for the service of the temple of the LORD is finished" (1 Chronicles 28:20). She was excited about the verse God gave her, and her mom crawled into bed with a glow in her heart, having been reminded again how ready Jessica is to leave our little nest. She is so ready because she knows the best place to go when she is anxious or fearful—to her Abba Father and His Word.

Boulder-Crushing God

On August 8 our Ben faced a major obstacle to getting into Auburn's Business School (closed out since February). God gave Ben some verses that morning from Psalm 2:7–9 assuring him of victory over the obstacle. As he drove to confront the obstacle, he was saying the verses over in his head when the accuser whispered, "Ben, those are great verses, but your doubts and your weak faith will cancel the promises God gave you." At that moment, Ben remembered what he had learned years ago in *Experiencing God* and realized this was a crisis of belief. He chose to believe what God said, and that day God crushed the boulder. Ben was admitted into Auburn. When he was driving home, he said to God, "I know any boulder I encounter in the future You will crush, and I will walk on crushed gravel." Ben said God's response was: "Ben, I will crush the boulders in your future and I will pick you up and carry you as I always have."

Oh, the tears that flowed that day as Ken and I listened to the living word Ben was given.

Ice Chips and Tonsils

When the date for Jessica's tonsillectomy arrived, my heart was a little anxious, but I kept telling myself this is a pretty routine surgery. My attitude reflected my lack of firsthand experience. An adult tonsillectomy is not a "routine" event. The physical suffering that followed left this mom pretty shocked.

Anyway, during one of the most difficult times, vomiting on a very sore throat, Jessica placed the most touching request. She whispered, "Mom, after you get me more ice chips, would you mind reading to me from Oswald Chambers' *My Utmost for His Highest?"* Jessica's request absolutely rocked my world. My child was very sick, yet her soul was coherent enough to request some soul food during such a physical struggle. As I held her and read to her, this mom's heart was blessed beyond words. My prayer that day was that difficult circumstances in Jessica's future would not dull her hunger for her life's greatest need—a daily dose of soul care.

Friends Like Daniel

While on vacation, I came upon Jessica and her friend Sandy looking at something very intensely. It was not a "hot" guy in a magazine or some cool outfit on the ideal model. Jessica was showing Sandy her latest gift from her parents: the Hebrew/Greek Word Study Bible. Jessica was showing Sandy how cool it is to look up key words in their original language and how wonderfully this enhances one's devotional time in the Word.

I walked away from the girls with the biggest grin on my face. Jessica said she wanted Sandy to go on vacation with us because she was the one friend she could freely share her heart with—a kindred spirit.

Today in my quiet time I found out that Daniel had three friends that we all need if we are going to live committed lives for Jesus. The original Hebrew names of Daniel's famous friends Shadrach, Meshach, and Abednego mean "The Lord is gracious," "The Lord is our helper," and "Who is like our God?" Don't we, like Daniel, need friends like these?

Parental Modeling 102

During Christmas, a friend of Jessica's said, "Jessie, whenever I spend time with you, you always make me want to go home and spend time with God in His Word." When I heard that remark, my heart just about exploded with joy.

Then today, Jessica told me that she had decided to start emailing her closest friends whenever the Lord gave her something particularly precious in her devotion time. She said she wanted to be an email cheerleader spiritually. Again my heart was flooded with joy since I, too, have been emailing my closest friends the special nuggets I have been mining from God's Word. During the last 22 years of parenting, I have known that modeling is more powerful than any well-thought-out parental sermon. In three weeks, I will be speaking to two thousand moms and teens at a conference in Austin. I plan to address the issue, "Is Mom modeling for her daughter the significance of a consistent, daily growing relationship with Jesus through God's Word?" I am going to ask each mother to think about what she is modeling as a priority in her daily life. Is she more concerned about the condition of her aging body than the care of her soul?

Tag Team for Jesus

Last weekend, Jessica and I went to a teen girls' conference in Austin, Texas. I asked Jessica before we left if she would be willing to share with a thousand teen girls why her daily quiet time in God's Word is so significant to her. I knew that the testimony of an older teen (19) to a younger teen would be most effective. I do not have the words to express the privilege of standing next to Jessica as we shared the microphone and I listened to her express her delight in her devotion to Christ. Jessica shared a cool quote from D. L. Moody: "The Scriptures were given not to increase our knowledge, but to change our lives."

As Jessica was talking, my mind flashed back to the very shy little girl that Jessica once was and the incredible conquering of her spirit of fear that has given her a courageous passion for Christ.

A couple hundred mothers were in the audience, and they were challenged to be the example they should be to their daughters in this most holy discipline of spending time in God's Word.

I don't know when the Lord will allow Jess and me to serve together again, but I must confess, it was too wonderful!

When Jess and I went back to the hotel room, she made an interesting comment. "Mom, it was so wonderful to share, but traveling to this conference was so draining, I don't think I could do this every weekend like you do." I grinned as Jessica got a glimpse of the price tag of traveling for Jesus. (Jessica and I have done ten conferences together since this first opportunity.)

Questions:
For Individual Reflection
or Group Study

1. Do you have a special place in your house where you have your daily time with God in His Word and prayer?
2. What keeps you from having at least seven minutes in the Word with God daily?
3. What method of Bible study do you use? What method has been the easiest for you?
4. When did you start establishing this "holy habit" in your life? (Luke 10:38-42)
5. Interact with M. E. Cravens' quote: "There is no success, no happiness, and no fulfillment in life apart from a consistent, daily growing relationship with Jesus through the Word."
6. Take a few moments to covenant with another believer to establish this holy habit of getting your seven minutes in the Word.
7. What translations of the Bible have been easier for you to comprehend?

Chapter 5

STAMP THE IMAGE OF
Emotional Health

**Principle:
A mentoring mom
cares for her own
emotional health.**

Perhaps one of the most powerful stamps that imprints upon your child's soul is that of your own soul's emotional health. Daily I stamp my children with the imprint of my soul's emotional condition, whether healthy or unhealthy. Whatever the degree of your own soul's health, you are stamping this imprint daily not only on your children but also on other people. I think about a mother's concern to keep her child away from the germs of another sick child, yet she doesn't protect her child from her own soul's germs.

Although much has been written about children carrying the pain of their parents, this area is often a blind spot for even the most educated Christians. It was just such a thought that provoked me to allow God to heal my heart wounds so that my children would not have to carry my pain. I wanted to break free from my painful past so that I could raise our children well.

Without question, a person can be a dedicated Christian but completely blind to her own heart wounds and the havoc they cause in the lives of those she loves. Let me share an example of such a blind spot in a parent's life. A mother was trying to help her daughter with her math homework. As the tension escalated between the mother and daughter, finally in frustration the mother screamed, "You are ruining my life and you're going to ruin my marriage!" To a ten-year-old girl, a mother screamed this accusation! The mother told this story at a Bible study and asked for prayer, because she said this child was driving her crazy. Now here is a very bright, college-educated woman who has known Jesus for many years. The issue is not the child; the child is really the mirror that reveals the mother's heart wound. Too often, the struggles with our children are not about them; instead these struggles are actually exposing our own internal war. Children are our mirrors, and often we do not appreciate the reflection that they reveal.

I have known this mother for years and her struggles started long before motherhood. Many years ago, this same woman shared some family struggles and the anger that was breaking her heart. I began praying for her that she would be delivered from anger's stronghold. From what she shared, I knew that she still had a snare in her soul from anger (Proverbs 22:24-25). Because this woman has not allowed God to heal the angry snare in her heart from her past, she is now stamping the angry wound on her child's heart. This little girl is likely to grow up and stamp a similar wound on her own child's heart. Knowing this vicious cycle, I tell moms all across our nation that if anybody ever suggests that you get professional help for your heart wounds—run to the phone today and make plans to start getting it!

I know from tough personal experience. Whenever you have a story about a princess, a wicked witch is usually on the horizon. I know that if I had not allowed the healing of my heart, I might have been the wicked witch hovering over our princess. I have met mothers who are jealous of their daughters. This jealousy is the reflection of unhealed heart wounds. One biblical definition of the word *jealousy* is "at war with the good in another." Dealing with the deprivation that I lived with as a child has kept me from being at war with the good in our princess's life. I have shed many tears of joy as I have witnessed the honor that our daughter has received from her father, brother, and friends.

Parents so often believe that a particular child *makes them angry*. They have varying names for such a child: high maintenance, strong-willed, more challenging. But often these parents need a tutorial in the area of anger. God helped me see that my own strong-willed child did not make me angry; rather my child exposed *my* anger. I learned through Dr. Ross Campbell's book *Kids in Danger* that I can't teach a child to handle his anger unless I have learned how to tame this destructive power in my own life.

Our stored anger can be referred to as "ancient anger." This ancient anger is like cobwebs in the attic of our heart. Frederick Buechner wrote about "ancient anger":

> Of the Seven Deadly Sins, anger is possibly the most fun. To lick your wounds, to smack your lips over grievances long past, to roll over your tongue the prospect of bitter confrontations still to come, to savor to the last toothsome morsel of both the pain you are given and the pain you are giving back—in many ways it is a feast fit for a king. The chief drawback is that what you are wolfing down is yourself. The skeleton you feast on is you.

Mom, it is time to place a phone call to the cleaning crew for the cobwebs of anger that are in the attic of your soul. This cleaning crew can be a pastor, a counselor, a Bible study leader, a Sunday school teacher, a prayer partner, or a spiritually mature friend.

Surrender Your Junior-God Badge

Another critical measurement of our soul's emotional health is our inclination to be controlling with our children. For many years, I wore what I've come to call a gigantic "junior-god badge" because I had an unhealthy commitment to controlling every aspect of my children's lives. Why was I so controlling? Why did I need a "junior-god badge" to match every outfit I wore?

Oswald Chambers wrote, "A Christian does not make much progress in spiritual maturity until he [she] realizes that life is more chaotic than predictable." The older I become, the more I realize that I cannot control my world; furthermore, the harder I try to control life, the more unpredictable it becomes! Accepting the reality behind Oswald Chambers' statement has actually brought my life more peace, even when things go crazy, when nothing is working out, when people around me are becoming anxious. I have removed my "junior-god badge," and I am taking early retirement from trying to control my part of the universe.

What fueled my propensity to be controlling? Quite simply it was the fear of pain. Pastor Steve Brown told me that "the source of most emotional and spiritual ills is an inappropriate effort to avoid pain." Because of my painful upbringing, I had an inordinate commitment not only to avoid pain in my life but to prevent it in my children's lives.

A life focused on preventing pain in my children's lives was one of the obvious manifestations of my deep heart wound. As we try to control everything in our children's lives, we become like *helicopter parents*. We parents who hover constantly overhead actually harm our children in our attempt to prevent them from being harmed. Our children grow up as anxious and frustrated as we are. Let Jesus heal you. Consider Barbara Sullivan's warning about this propensity to control, "Control is an outgrowth of fear, insecurity and lack of self-esteem. The more anxious a woman is the more she wants to control and conversely, the more secure a woman is, the less likely she will need to control."

The worst aspect of being a controlling mother is the fear that pulsates through your body daily. An older man rebuked my fear concerning our son. I was fearfully trying to control every aspect of his life, and consequently

I was living in a graceless condition. Al said to me, "Jackie, God does not give grace for 'hypothetical' situations." Grace is only for reality, not fearful illusions. Fear is False Evidence Appearing Real. Fear about something painful happening to one's child is a fear without grace. My fear kept me from believing that God's grace is sufficient (2 Corinthians 12:9).

When our children were in elementary school, my sister Bobbie killed herself. My good friend Liz suggested that I see a professional Christian counselor. My immediate response was defensive. I remember asking, "Why do I have to go again? I have already seen a great Christian counselor about the sexual abuse I faced as a child and a teen." Her response was, "Jackie, you need to look a little more closely at the family you grew up in and the family that helped impact Bobbie's suicide." Liz could see my resistance to her suggestion (since she also was a professional counselor). So Liz wisely pulled out the trump card and said, "OK, if you won't go for yourself, go for your children. Don't make them live through whatever you've lived through that would allow a sibling to kill herself." For the sake of my children, I called for the appointment with a Christian counselor. That counseling revealed a deep blind spot that I was carrying in my soul. (Sadly, four years later, my brother Johnny killed himself.)

Gary Smalley said, "Going through harrowing experiences as a family draws people together like nothing else. In other words, the real secret to becoming a close-knit family is shared experiences that turn into shared trials." Our children have become compassionate young adults through the grief that has broken their hearts.

Stop Trying to Please Everybody

During this particular time of counseling, a good friend mailed me a copy of the book *Search for Significance*. This book was liberating to me. So many moms live with the bondage of trying to measure up to everyone else's opinion of them. Through this book I discovered that I don't have to tap dance to please everybody and that other people are not my judges. They might look like my judges, but I live and die unto Jesus, and He's crazy about me!

People pleasing has a stranglehold on so many mothers. They actually correct their children for the sake of those watching rather than for the good of the child. I have seen mothers press their sharp fingernails into the arms of their wiggling child, not because the mother was concerned about the child hearing the sermon but because she was concerned about Deacon So-and-So sitting directly behind her. She assumed that the deacon was evaluating her parenting skills. It is hard enough for most adults to sit still through a long sermon, much less a young child.

I know that I lived with that type of "taskmaster" bondage for several years. A mother's people pleasing is deadly; it is like inhaling a mouthful of sawdust. After good counsel and reading several grace-filled books (consult the suggested reading list in the back of this book), I realized that for several years I had been parenting our children with a grievous heart wound. Consequently, when our children reached their teens I told each of them, "If you ever feel you need to talk to someone about growing up with a mom who was not healed completely, it's OK." I have given both our children permission to evaluate an upbringing that was less than perfect with such a controlling, fearful mom.

Several times I have told our firstborn, "Go get all the help you need, sweetheart, because I know how blind I was as a mom when you were young." I reassured him that he would not dishonor me by discussing with a counselor how controlling I was at times. I told Ben that the word *honor* in Hebrew means "measure weight of influence," and sometimes the weight of influence has not been positive. I humbly own that as a parent so that my child is free to look at his own heart wounds.

I think all parents should put aside money in a savings account for their firstborn child. This money is not for college or their future wedding. This money is for the counseling the firstborn child will need since the first one is the child that the parents *practiced* their shallow parenting skills on.

A decade ago, I met a woman who had a wounded heart, but either she did not know it or she was doing her best to cover it up (great clothes, fine jewelry, etc.). Deep pain in the life of her child helped convince her to go to a Christian counselor. She went to the counselor with the agenda to get her child help; in the process, she discovered the key to her own issues! She began bravely looking at her wounds and letting Jesus heal the hurt and anger.

This mom told me yesterday at lunch that the best thing she could do for her daughter is to let Jesus heal her wounded heart. A promise for mother and daughter: "Do not be afraid; you will not suffer shame. Do not fear disgrace; you will not be humiliated. You will forget the shame of your youth" (Isaiah 54:4).

As a young mom, I lived breathlessly trying to measure up to the perfect mom ideal. I was trying to live up to everybody else's expectations, but then I found out that I was completely in bondage to people and not to God. "Am I now trying to win the approval of men, or of God? Or am I trying to please men? If I were still trying to please men, I would not be a servant of Christ" (Galatians 1:10).

Another aspect of my blind spot was my response to the instruction of other Christians. Too often when an older godly woman spoke, I would think, *She must be speaking for God.* Then as a serious student of God's Word, I became more discerning about what I heard and what I incorporated in my parenting style. When I was a young mom and heard a speaker start expressing the "ten commandments for the perfect mom," I was intimidated by such ideals. The more mature I became spiritually and emotionally, the more I was able to differentiate between ideals and reality. In fact, a woman would be teaching on the ideal mom and I would get this holy nudge in my heart, "Excuse me, that is not from the Holy One, that is merely your opinion of parenting."

When you realize some of the lies you grew up believing, you can stop the cycle. You will become more intentional about telling yourself the truth and living that truth. "Then you will know the truth, and the truth will set you free" (John 8:32). "Your Word is truth" (John 17:17). Replace the lies with the truth of God's Word. Rick Warren, author of *The Purpose Driven Life*, said,

"The Christian life is the process of replacing lies with the truth." Don't let your children grow up believing the same lies that your parents raised you to embrace. We need to allow for the proper care of our souls so that our children will be healthy enough emotionally to pursue God's purpose for them.

Recently through premarital counseling, our son made the difficult decision to break his engagement. What was the key to the courage to make such a difficult decision? The counselor asked Ben what he wanted in a marriage and he said, "I want a marriage like my parents have." Then the counselor asked him if he could have such a marriage with his fiancée. The answer came with tears and the ultimate decision to break his engagement. Now, do Ken and I have the perfect marriage? Absolutely not; but we do have a marriage where open communication, honesty, love, and forgiveness are common characteristics. We as a family have learned that we are as sick as our secrets. Recently a dear friend who is a college minister described our family as four passionate communicators. In an article in *Psychology for Living*, Bruce Narramore made this statement: "Admitting our imperfections sets a tone of mutual respect that goes a long way in promoting good parent-child relations."

Another aspect of stamping our soul's emotional health on our children is demonstrating how to be a great forgiver. I am often amazed that parents can be so thorough in teaching their children about hygiene but neglect the hygiene of the soul. Parents will harp on children to brush and floss their teeth but allow a child to grind his teeth in anger toward a sibling. The soul is cleansed and "flossed" when a person has the freedom to admit failure and ask forgiveness. I am always asking parents, "When was the last time you admitted you were wrong and asked your child or mate for forgiveness?" Ruth Graham said years ago, "A good marriage is made up of two good forgivers."

Playfully Celebrate Your Differences

Often opposites are attracted to each other—and then they marry. That which was the source of attraction can change into a source of irritation. Ken and I have spent 30 years trying to understand each other. We have not always been very successful. I always knew that our success with understanding each other would eventually parallel our understanding of our children. I knew in my heart that the places where Ken and I are stuck in our differences would be the exact places we would end up stuck in trying to understand our children. The teen years exposed some painful areas of Ken's and my differences. The good news is that we got good counsel from those who are much wiser than we are. This counsel has resulted in some obvious changes in our home, which can be summarized by simply saying that the very qualities that used to be "attacked" around our home have now become reason for playful celebration. Ken and Ben started going to lunch twice a week, and with all those luncheons came an understanding that released this playful celebration between them. This quote captures what I have seen: "I ask you to understand me. That will come only when you are willing to give up changing me into a copy of you."

God has been teaching Ken and me that our children are God's masterpieces (Ephesians 2:10) and not ours. Ken and I heard the most liberating statement in Atlanta. We were standing in a parking lot talking with a good friend when he said, "You realize, don't you, that God did not call you to rear godly children; He called you to be godly parents."

Parents are often so focused on their children doing well in school because they assume that will assure a great future. I know hundreds of students who have passed school but flunked life. Parents spend hours coaching their children in various sports but completely neglect coaching them how to be good forgivers. Teaching them to be a good forgiver is a great legacy to give every child. A child who knows how to ask forgiveness and how to give forgiveness will be a pleasure to be around. Quoting her late mother in an article in *Real Life* magazine, Karen Bradford wrote: "It's good to be smart, but it's better to get along. If people like having you around, your life will be a whole lot easier."

When I was raising our children, I was very intentional about teaching and demonstrating people skills so that our children would be a welcome sight when they went into the homes of others. I prayerfully raised children who would be invited back to a friend's home. For seven years my husband and I taught a Bible study for the Montreal Expos and Atlanta Braves during spring training. We had many players come to our home for dinner. After spending time with our children they often remarked, "Do you guys rent your kids out? We would love to have them for a summer!"

One day after a very long phone call, Ben came out of his room and said, "I am so excited that this good friend of mine is coming to visit us over the Memorial Day weekend." We asked, "Why?" Ben's immediate remark was, "Our home is the perfect place for him to come, because our loving family is exactly what a wounded heart needs." How thrilled Ken and I were to hear Ben's comment. We have always desired our home to be a safe place where God's grace can be displayed and shared freely.

Is your home a safe place for a weary heart? I have been in some homes where a weary soul would experience "dis-grace" rather than God's extravagant healing grace.

Application: The Stamp of Your Soul's Health

You Are the Rose

In the seventies, a friend of mine made an unforgettable remark to me as she was leaving my home after spending an evening with my dysfunctional family. She said, "Jackie, you are a pearl in a pile of garbage." When the patriarch of my dysfunctional family died without Jesus, a dear friend wrote this poem for my devastated heart. Instead of describing me as a pearl, this friend saw me as a rose.

You Are the Rose

*You are the blossom, you are the rose
That has come through a lineage of thorns.
You are the treasure, you are the prose,
Your words are perfume to the soul,*

*You are the rose.
The thorns you have come through
Have brought much pain,
And there are tears on your blossoms,
As you have walked through the rain.
The vine that you came from has been cut down,
But the seed you have grown from
Has become a golden crown.*

*May the Son whose light sustains you
Hold you securely through this storm,
And may His love surround you
And keep you warm.*

*Your seeds that are planted
Far and wide on this ground,
Will fill the world with roses
All from the vine cut down.*

—Janet Falkman

Healthy Soul, Through Honest Grief

One day in the grocery store, Jessica said, "Mommy, with every passing Christmas our family shrinks. First, we lost Aunt Bobbie, then Grandpa, then Uncle Mark, and now my favorite cousin, Jennifer, has moved far away." She started to cry and I just hugged her and cried with her in front of the Frosted Flakes. I am so grateful for the lessons I have learned through healthy grief. I have learned that tears do not bring back the one who has died, but tears bring us back to the life that must be lived without the ones who have died. Certain songs, pictures, and occasions during the holidays have brought our family tears, but we know tears are normal for those of us who have suffered loss.

We have been comforted by the following passage: "And provide for those who grieve in Zion—to bestow on them a crown of beauty instead of ashes, the oil of gladness instead of mourning, and a garment of praise instead of a spirit of despair. They will be called oaks of righteousness, a planting of the LORD" (Isaiah 61:3).

Emotional Bonding Thanksgiving

Today we are leaving for a Thanksgiving camping trip. Camping and hunting—a first for the Ken Kendall Family. This is going to be one of the greatest challenges for the oldest member of our family (me—I am eight days older than Ken). To me, camping is Hampton Inn. Gary Smalley constantly refers to the "emotional bonding" that a family experiences while camping. Right now that phrase seems more like "emotional bombing" to me. Everyone keeps telling me that we are going to have such a great time! I want to believe, so I am packing the bug spray and ponchos by faith!

Emotional "Bonding" or "Bombing"?

Many friends and family members called to find out how the Kendalls did camping. Everyone expected our camping adventure to be the "emotional bombing" I had feared. How shocked each caller was to find out that we had a great time—the "emotional bonding" overpowered any "bombs" we encountered.

After several hours of hunting with no success, the men and dogs had gone into a thickly wooded area in hopes of finding a wild pig. We heard the dogs start barking—not the typical barking of the neighborhood dog on the one morning you could sleep in past 7:00 A.M., but the barking that signals discovery. The women and little girls on the swamp buggy started to squeal with excitement. Suddenly out of the thick trees and bushes came a wild pig. Three dogs were close behind, then Danny running with the gun, then Ben running behind Danny. Behind this excited caravan was Ken Kendall running with a video camera in hand, trying to capture this moment on film. Danny's mom yelled when she saw Ken, "Who does Ken think he is—Walter Cronkite of Wild Kingdom?"

Driving back to camp, a beautiful sunset was on our left, a full moon had already risen on our right, and a wonderful breeze blew across this wide open plain. As we laughed and sang and rehearsed the day's hunting adventure, I finally understood the emotional bonding that camping/hunting provides.

Later we had our Thanksgiving dinner in the woods. Words are inadequate to describe the unspeakable blessings of family, friends, and a heavenly Father who enjoys our bonding with one another in Him. There is a record in heaven of our conversations around the picnic table in the woods that Thanksgiving. "Then those who feared the LORD talked with each other, and the LORD listened and heard. A scroll of remembrance was written in his presence concerning those who feared the LORD and honored his name" (Malachi 3:16).

O.B. Mom Hazardous to Teens' Health

Having had the privilege of being a stay-at-home mom, I have enjoyed the many ways that I am always able to be there for our children. Lately, I have been having the most difficult time being weaned from being needed—my teenagers just don't need me so much anymore. Of course, I know that they still need a mom, but I have really struggled with letting go of certain things that I must release if Ben and Jessica are going to walk responsibly with their God. Ben and I have had many "heated" discussions this summer over my being O.B. These initials are a code for my too often controlling tendency that results in Mom being overbearing!

I want Ben to be the man that God desires—and I am painfully aware of the ways I can stand in Ben's way in my O.B. sort of way. I am praying to learn to release Ben and Jessica to their God-ordained scripts—scripts written by a heavenly Father rather than a controlling mother.

Emotional Checklist

The night before the new school year began, we took our teens out to dinner to discuss the ending of summer vacation and the beginning of a new school year. We decided to take Ben and Jessica through a little "checklist" survey of the characteristics of the successful family (from Jay Kesler's material). Of course, we waited till they had finished eating before we began asking their critique of our family. As we went through each characteristic, here are some of their responses:

Families That Succeed

1. Where love is openly evident between husband and wife.
   Jessica:"There is plenty and we don't need more!"
2. Where respect for each individual is insured.
   Jessica: "If it wasn't, we would want to change mom!"
3. Where rules and boundaries are understood and communicated.
   Ben and Jessica:Very clear. (Ken didn't agree with their judgment, he feels we are sometimes vague rule-wise. The kids disagreed.)
4. Where problems are confronted openly and given proper weight.
   Ben and Jessica: Dad is a great balance for Mom when she is overbearing, and Mom sometimes has to balance Dad's overreacting.
5. Where all in the home are committed to process.
   Ben:"We are so wonderful, why we're the freakin' Brady Bunch!" (Ben's remark caused such laughter that we almost did not get to number 6.)
6. Where Christ is at the head of not only the children, but also everybody.
   Ben:"Obviously..."

Just Parents

Recently, I was chatting with a girl and telling her I had been praying for her. I told her how concerned I had been for her, knowing that her parents had moved away and she stayed behind with another family to complete her senior year. As I expressed my concern for her, she said something that blew me away. She said, "I'm OK, Mrs. Kendall. My parents—well, they're 'just parents'—we aren't close like you are with your children. I never saw very much of them because they both work so much. You are close to your kids, like friends, whereas my parents—they're 'just parents.'" I drove away from that young woman with tears in my eyes.

Common Stumbling Block for Loving Parents

Tonight I was breaking a rule I made. In fact, this rule is taped to my kitchen cabinet and I typed it, yet I was breaking it. The rule says: "Refuse to nag." Well, I was nagging Ben about his being gone all day when he was going out of town the next day. I told him that I was nagging him because I missed him so much. Then Ben said something that made me laugh and stop nagging. He said, "Mom, you spent plenty of time with me when I was younger." Ouch! His comment made me think of something I had just underlined in the book *Give Them Wings*: "If family is a priority and we eagerly pour ourselves into the lives of one another, watching kids pull away from us and get ready to leave home is very difficult. *The closeness we've created becomes the stumbling block we have to crawl over in the adjustment*" (italics added).

Ken and I have scraped our knees crawling over this "stumbling block." We are learning how to be observers more often and stage directors less often. Recently, Ben gave his girlfriend a verse for confidence as she tried out for club volleyball. "Because the Sovereign LORD helps me, I will not be disgraced. Therefore have I set my face like flint, and I know I will not be put to shame" (Isaiah 50:7). Lisa wrote the verse on the inside of each of her kneepads! Ben and Lisa write key verses that they find during their daily devotions on 3-by-5-inch cards and they carry them in their pockets to school and then compare notes over the phone after school. I asked Ben why he shaves at night. He said, "So I have more time for devotions in the morning!" Well, I guess the observer position rather than stage director does not seem so bad, after all.

Introverts: Treasures to Be Discovered

The other night, Jessica asked if I could type some poems for her while she went to play practice. The following was the first of ten poems:

She looks into the mirror and sees her reflection:
She also sees such imperfection,
There she stands gazing into the mirror

The world around her thinks she is secure;
They don't seem to know the real her,
Slowly she takes a stumbling fall.

As I continued to type poems she had written, I had to stop and go find Ben and show him the treasure of poetry I was typing. When he finished reading all her poems, he said, "Where did these come from?" Then Ben and I discussed how "inside people" are treasures to be discovered. We were thrilled to catch another glimpse of the princess who is living in our house.

Love Notes on Doorframes

A couple of weeks ago, when Ben came in from a date with his girlfriend, he went straight to the den and turned the computer on. This was not typical; he usually goes straight to the refrigerator and then to the couch where he chats with us about the evening. I went into the den and asked Ben what he was doing and he said, "Mom, I'll tell you when I am finished typing." He came out of the den with a pile of papers, but I knew he hadn't typed that many pages. Then he told me what he had done. Someone had hurt his girlfriend's feelings. After she shared her heart with him, he came home and designed a flyer that declared how precious she was to God and him. He ran 14 copies of the flyer and told me that he was going to get up early and go over to Lisa's house and tape the 14 flyers to her front door. When Lisa got up to go take her finals, she would see the declarations of Ben's encouragement and love all over her front door!

Needless to say, I was deeply moved by Ben's gesture of love. His brainstorm brought to my mind so many loving things Ken has done for me since we began dating in 1973. What an awesome example and model Ken has been for our son. Then the Lord reminded me of a biblical parallel of Ben's gesture of love: "These commandments that I give you today are to be upon your hearts.... Write them on the *doorframes* of your houses and on your gates" (Deuteronomy 6:6, 9 italics added). We have a chance daily to write the good news of God's love on the *doorframes of people's lives*, not least of which, our own children's lives.

Captivity

Sometimes I feel that I am a captive of my weakness as a parent. My lack of courage had only intensified this sense of captivity until recently when the Lord showed me that I can be fruitful and I need not let a single day dwindle away focused on my inadequacies. Therefore, when I feel I am in captivity, I can glorify Him. "To all the captives he has exiled to Babylon.... Build homes, and plan to stay. Plant gardens, and eat the food you produce. Marry, and have children. Then find spouses for them and have many grandchildren. Multiply! *Do not dwindle away*" (Jeremiah 29:4-6, italics added).

We do not have to let one day in the next year dwindle away. Build...plant...garden...eat...multiply!

Are You a Whiner or Worshipper?

While doing some last-minute tasks before leaving for a five-day conference, I was standing knee deep in dirty clothes very late at night. Everyone had gone to bed and I felt a "tude" (attitude) coming on. I paused and resisted whining and said to Jesus, "Please show me how to worship You even in a laundry room." Suddenly, I had this thought: *Give thanks for each person that the dirty clothes represent.* As I began to sort the clothes, I gave thanks for Ken, Ben, and Jessica. As I gave thanks, my heart began to overflow with joy and praise for our Lord. Then I remembered a definition of worship— "thanks that can't be constrained." I got so excited thinking about worshipping Jesus even in our laundry room!

The next day, as I was finishing up all the final details before leaving, I realized that I had forgotten one more thing, which would require another trip to the drugstore. As I was driving to the store in a horrible rainstorm, I could feel the stress increasing and I was struggling with a huge urge to whine. I began to pray and ask Jesus to again show me how to worship (give thanks) even in the car in a rainstorm on the way to the store. Resisting the urge to whine, by faith I gave thanks to God for another last-minute trip. Suddenly I was overpowered with God's peace. As I walked from aisle to aisle, I noticed that stress was gone and that joy began to fill my heart. Approaching the counter to pay, I noticed a long line and just grinned as I stood there filled with peace.

While I was standing in line, I noticed that the cashier (Teresa) seemed a little disoriented and wasn't acting like her normal, friendly self. I also noticed that she was sweating profusely although the store was not hot. As her disorientation increased, suddenly I called out, "Teresa, are you all right?" She looked at me, her eyes full of panic, and exclaimed, "I am a diabetic, and I didn't get my break. My cheese and juice are in my car." Well, immediately I got out of line, ran to get some orange juice out of the case, came to her side, and gave her the juice, telling her to drink it *now*. She drank the whole container and then reached out her arms to hug me. I hugged her back. She began to cry and said, "God sent you into this store." My reply: "You've got that right!" I know that if I had rushed into the store, stressed out and whining to myself,

I would never have noticed the condition of a needy diabetic named Teresa.

I am so excited about learning the passwords of praise that can transform a laundry room or a trip to the store into a chapel filled with praise. These passwords of praise flow from the heart when a person practices: "Give thanks in all circumstances, for this is God's will for you in Christ Jesus" (1 Thessalonians 5:18). A thankful heart is a component of one's emotional health.

Sexual Abuse Redeemed

Recently while taking Jessica to a doctor's appointment, Ben called me and said, "Mom, where are you? I need you to come home now." My first thought when I heard his urgency was, *He must have had a car accident!* But when I asked Ben what was wrong, he said, "Nothing is wrong, but I need you to come home because we have someone at the house that you need to talk to." Ben and two friends had been sharing Jesus with a classmate and he suggested bringing her over to our house where they could finish sharing with her and maybe his mom could add a few helpful comments.

I told Ben I wouldn't be home for at least another hour and I was sure they were doing a great job sharing Jesus. Ben told me that he had told the teenager (Patty) that his mom had a bad background, but that Jesus brought good out of a difficult family life. Then later that day, Ben had the privilege of leading Patty in the sinner's prayer, and she committed her life to Jesus. I was telling a spiritual mentor about Ben's opportunity and my mentor said, "I bet you would never have dreamed that God would so effectively use your difficult background in so many wonderful ways! God not only uses your difficult family upbringing to bless people in conferences but God also allows Ben to use your testimony to witness to teenagers from difficult families."

We know that God brings beauty from ashes. I am so grateful that the effect of His healing touch reaches not only me but also teenagers that Ben and Jessica can encourage because they have seen the context of ashes in their mom's painful past and the hope of beauty in Jesus (Isaiah 61:1–7). God has brought so many wounded teens into our children's lives and they have told them that they know God can bring good out of evil, even the evil of abuse. Such confident sharing comes from their being stamped with the image of the healing of a wounded heart.

Mom, Go to Your Room

The summer of 1998 has been harder than ever for this mom. One day I was so-o-o-o-o cranky that while driving in my car, I was whining like a baby. Then I heard in my heart this phrase, *Go to your room.* At first I smiled thinking the Lord was telling me to go to my room. Then I realized that His tough love was a compassionate love. He was trying to spare me having one of my teenagers pushed to the edge by an unbearably cranky mom. I literally went to my room for the rest of the afternoon. As I cleaned out my closet and dresser drawers, the Lord began to clean my heart from the faithless crankiness. Some days each of us would be better off if we went to our rooms and didn't come out until we are kind enough to face another soul.

During this difficult time, the Lord used Ann Kiemel Anderson (one of my favorite authors in college) to comfort my exhausted cranky heart! The following quote expresses my conclusion (now that I am allowed out of my room): "It feels right to me that life must have balance. That good times and hard times are meticulously measured out, for it is only in the blend of both that we grow...that wholeness comes. We know how to laugh with others and how to cry. Substance in the human heart is built...nurtured...so much more by pain and failure and disappointment than by happiness and joy (Biblical principle: Ecclesiastes 7:2-3).

A Real Princess

For all the romantics out there and for all the skeptics who think chivalry is dead, early in the morning on Jessica's 17th birthday, a young man placed yellow roses in the shape of a star on the front of Jessica's car. In the center of the roses was the verse Daniel 12:3. Jessica was impressed; her mom was blown away. Then I realized that Jessica's calmer response was the result of years of being treated like a princess not only by her daddy but also by her big brother. With her senior year almost here, we are cherishing every moment parenting our princess. Her junior year has been the most demanding and most fun. Jessica expects to be treated with honor, like a princess. PS: Sometimes I have been concerned that our "princess" will never find a prince of a guy in the 21st century. I have wondered if anyone would understand the high standard of honor Jessica has lived with. Well, in the spring of 2003, her prince arrived. Jessica's first compliment of her prince was, "The way Drew treats me reminds me of the way Dad and Ben have always treated me."

Emotional Heirlooms

How I praise God for all the wise parents who time and again reminded me to cherish all my "mommy moments" throughout the years. I did my best to pay close attention to these gifts of connecting time with our children during the last two decades. What I did not realize until recently is that those many mom/dad moments become cherished memories when our children leave home—emotional heirlooms. We have all been challenged to cherish the time we have with our children, but sometimes we allow the busyness of our lives to make our relationships with our children a little barren. Making time to connect heart to heart with one's child will provide emotional heirlooms rather than the trunkloads of regret and guilt of lost opportunities. Mom/dad moments cannot be recaptured, and such heirlooms are not available on back order. Recently, Ken and I have been paging through the emotional heirlooms that fill the scrapbooks of our hearts. Just the other night I thanked Ken for working so hard so we could have two decades of emotional heirlooms that we are both cherishing as our nest empties.

Forever grateful for the
Two precious birds who have
Dwelt in our nest...
We by faith entrust
Them to a Sovereign Soaring Eagle—
As they leave our nest.

New Definition for Birthdays

Recently Jessica was talking with Ben on the phone about being "so busy" that she wasn't sure if she would be able to drive to Atlanta to celebrate his 22nd birthday. As she was trying to explain to Ben all that she had to do that weekend, Ben replied, "Jessica, do you know what birthday celebrations are for? They are for people who don't know they are loved every other day of the year…and Jessica, I know how much you love me." Ben's remark not only touched Jessica, but also her mom and dad when she called us and told us what Ben said. What Ben did not know was his little sister was rambling to fool him into thinking she was not going to drive to Atlanta and surprise him for his birthday. Jessica and Ben's friends had been planning for weeks for Jessica to come to Atlanta and surprise her brother on his birthday. Ben and Jessica's love for each other is one of the greatest gifts to Ken and me.

Often in a dysfunctional family, siblings are alienated from each other through the heart wounds that are experienced in the family's context. I do not take for granted the loving relationship between our children. I am the oldest of seven children, and I grew up isolated from my siblings as we each did what we could to survive our dysfunctional home. Our unhealthy survival techniques produced a Grand Canyon of distance between each of us.

We're Not Doing This Again

When our kids were home for spring break in March, we had to tell them that they would not be able to fly home for Easter, and they both seemed totally at peace with this situation. The week before Easter, Ben and Jess called each other and began to discuss how they could actually get home for Easter and then make it back to school in time for their classes. They would drive round trip 26 hours and they would be home for less than 36 hours. Well, when they told us their idea we said no. Since they both received invitations to visit with other closer families for Easter, we had peace. On Easter Sunday, driving back from dinner with friends, Ben called home and said, "We are not doing this next year. When the Kendalls gather for a celebration, Jess and I want to be there." Ben and Jess's love for their family is an awesome gift of joy for Ken and me.

The Kendall family as a whole has been through times of soul searching and healing, especially after the death of two precious family members. Our family gatherings have become more than just a joyful time, but they are also an emotionally safe time. I believe our grown children's desire to be at Kendall family gatherings is not simply because of the good food and laughter but also the soul food that is available.

Questions:
For Individual Reflection
or Group Study

1. What do you think about the statement: "If I don't let God heal my heart wounds, then my children will carry my pain"? (Psalm 26:2; 34:18-19)

2. Do you have a challenging child who may be a mirror of your own needs? (1 Corinthians 13:11-12; Ephesians 6:4)

3. Do you have a "junior-god badge" you need to surrender? (Genesis 3:16b; Psalm 115:3; Jonah 2:8; 1 John 5:23)

4. Would your children consider you to be an overbearing mom? (Proverbs 14:1; 24:3-4)

5. Is your home a safe place for struggling souls? (Isaiah 61:1-7; Luke 4:18-19)

6. Have you been courageous enough to get counsel for areas you are struggling with as a mother? (Isaiah 26:3; 1 Thessalonians 5:23; 3 John 2)

7. Would your children describe you as a "whiner" or a "worshipper"? (1 Thessalonians 5:18)

Chapter 6

STAMP THE IMAGE OF
Loving People to Christ

 **Principle:
Your children deliver
your mission field
to your front door.**

Y ou as a mom are one of God's greatest secret weapons! How strategically you have been placed in your sphere of influence! Each child that your child brings into your home is a mission field for you. As a mom, you get to stamp the image of a mom loving people to Christ (2 Corinthians 5:17–20). As my kids would say, "Mom, that is a no-brainer."

Steven Curtis Chapman is my favorite Christian performing artist. On one of his CDs, he sings a phrase that captures this particular mentoring stamp. He sings, "We love God best when we love each other well." You and I have loved

God best when we have loved each child our children deliver to our homes. How much do you love God? How would the friends of your children answer that question concerning you? How would the parents of your children's friends respond to that question? Before we proceed any further, be aware that this assignment is not just for moms but also grandmoms. I have met hundreds of young people who have been profoundly impacted with the love of God through their "mentoring" grandmothers.

Your children will attract a variety of young people who end up in your living room. When the mission field comes through your door, you may be tempted to say, "Oh no, I don't like that boy," or, "I don't like that girl." Reflect before you respond. Be careful not to reject any child so quickly. These young ones have been delivered into your home by the Holy One. God knew they were going to meet you and that you were going to stamp the love of God on them. Your human response may be, "Not this type of child, Lord! Isn't it time for him to go home?" You cannot love your kids' friends to Jesus without accepting them where they are and praying for where they need to go. When you accept where they are and pray for where they need to go, then you have effectively fulfilled your place in this mission field that God delivered to your living room.

One of the cards in my little prayer roll-a-dex (described in chapter 3) is called the "God Squad" card, and on that card I put the name of every teenager that God ever brought into my life through our two children. I did not put them on the card because they *are* part of the local God Squad (local teens making a difference for

Jesus). I put them on that prayer card list *believing* that someday, if I pray faithfully for them, God is going to capture their hearts and transform them into blazing torches for God's glory.

When our kids were in junior high and high school, I may have looked pretty foolish to some people watching me loving on kids who were less than perfect. In fact, I know that some of the teens thought I was absolutely clueless about their poor choices. These teens would assume I didn't know the truth about them because I so loved them. As the teenagers came to learn about how much I knew, they were stunned that I treated them so lovingly. I knew that as a follower of Jesus, if I didn't love these teens, they would have a difficult time believing that the God they cannot see loves them. If we don't love people, they'll never believe that God does.

Then, after I was able to win their respect because I unconditionally loved, them I was then able to speak the truth to them. I spent many nights talking to young people in my home about such topics as alcohol and moral purity. This platform from which I spoke was built with bricks of love, and these bricks of love were made with hours of listening and baking many pans of brownies for a captive audience in my family room. This is why quantity time is as significant as quality time with teenagers. You can't schedule quality time with teens without the preface of quantity time.

Spiritual Surrogate Mom

So often in the last decade, I have heard this generation mentioning the principle of "earning the right to be heard." As a mom of teens, this principle is so true, but its application is often not possible with busy lifestyles. Earning the right to be heard takes so much time. Maybe that is one of the reasons for the communication gap between generations. Ironically, a woman is given maternity leave when she has a newborn because this is such a critical bonding time. Yet I see the lack of bonding between parents and their teens, so maybe some teens' parents need to apply for a leave of absence to connect with their teens.

I was a spiritual surrogate mom to many of these young people. I have been called "Mom Number 2" by several young people that I have loved on, cheered on, cried with, and even argued with a few times. I discovered this year that the great apostle Paul had a spiritual surrogate mom: "Greet Rufus, chosen in the Lord, and his mother, *who has been a mother to me, too*" (Romans 16:13, italics added).

Even Paul, a grown man, needed a "mother." Instead of viewing additional young people in your home as a burden, ask the Lord to help you see them as a gift because your ministry in their lives is not only a gift to their hearts; it is also a gift to *your* heart.

One day while reading in the book of Numbers, I came across a fresh perspective on such serving. I was reminded of the awesome privilege of serving and the gift it was to my life. "I am giving you service of the priesthood *as a gift to you*" (Numbers 18:7, italics added).

The moment I read that, a thought flowed into my heart. *Service is not a gift we give God, but a gift He gives us.* The current view of Christian service is something that we "give" to God or something that we "do" for God. We applaud people who serve God in all the various ministries that exist today. We are impressed when people decide to use a week of their vacation to go on a mission trip. After reading this verse, I realized that going on short-term mission trips, working at a soup kitchen on Saturday mornings, teaching a home Bible study, visiting people in nursing homes, helping with handicapped children, giving money to ministries so they can be more fruitful...all these acts of service are just believers opening gifts that God gave them.

Ken and I have been involved in some form of ministry since 1969, and today I realized as never before what an awesome gift from God ministry has been to our lives. Did you do something for Jesus today or this week or this month? Your service was God's gift to you, not your gift to God. *Being a spiritual surrogate mother is a gift to your heart from God to be embraced and opened with joy.*

Amy Carmichael was a spiritual surrogate mother to many while she served as a missionary in India. Her life story inspired me to make a difference in "my India." One of her quotes that motivated me as a young mother was "Although He knew that we would never comprehend the height or depth or length or breadth of His love, nevertheless He went to the Cross, bearing our sins. Oh, that we might know Calvary's love." Calvary's love motivated me when I wanted to close the door on one more child who needed my love and attention for the sake of the cross.

The young people on my "God Squad" prayer card are now in college or grad school. Lately I have been running across young people who keep mentioning various young men and women my kids knew in high school, and one remark keeps coming up again and again. The common remark is, "Mrs. Kendall, _____ is doing so well; you would be so impressed." I always smile and say, "You know, that is what I have been praying for—for several years."

I have been noticing a harvest full of answers to prayer concerning the young people who were delivered to my family room through our children. Some of these young people went off to college where they played the games, did the dance, chased the illusions, and have discovered only an inconsolable ache. When they discovered how empty the darkness is, guess who they have called for answers!

When one boy called late one night my husband said, "Who is this and whom do you want to speak with?" He knew the young man, but was shocked that he asked to speak with "Mrs. Kendall." Ken told the young man that I was at a speaking engagement and that he needed to call back after 10 P.M. When I got home and my husband told me who had called, I just smiled, because this young man was one of the rowdy boys from high school whom I happen to know everything about and have been praying for—for years. Before he called back, I prayed and asked the Lord to keep me in a *place* of love first and preaching second. So when the phone finally rang, I calmly said, "Hi, how's it going? How's college?" (I can imagine.) And he said, "Um, Mrs. Kendall, I need to talk to you about God and women." I said, "Well, those are two of my favorite topics." What followed was one of the most amazing answers to prayer I have ever had from my "God Squad" card.

We discussed the girl he was dating and his need to break up with her because she was not a Christian. He asked me for the title of a good book that would help his girlfriend understand the depth of the differences between their faiths—even if he had not walked in what he was raised believing. I told him to get her a copy of the book *A Case for Christ*, and I asked him a couple questions in relation to his girlfriend's faith. He mentioned that she was Jewish. I answered several questions about the gap between their faiths, reassuring him that if he gets flustered when trying to communicate the difference between their faiths, he should say that he can't explain it all but the book he is giving her will answer many of her questions about Jesus.

Just before the end of our conversation I said to him, "If you want to give her my email address, I would be glad to answer any of her questions concerning Jesus really being Messiah." Within a couple days of that phone call, I got this email: "My boyfriend has just broke up with me. He said I should email you if I have any questions about the book I am reading, *A Case for Christ*." I invited her to meet me for dinner where, for three hours, I answered many questions. The first question out of her mouth after we ordered dinner was, "Why do you think the Jews rejected the Messiah?" My response: "I wonder how late this restaurant is open—for that explanation!"

Before I had left to meet her for dinner, the Lord brought to my mind, "New Bible and Post-it notes."

During the three hours that we talked, every time she asked me a question, I would find a verse in the Bible to answer her and would mark the verse, placing a sticky note on the page. I told her that I wanted her to have answers from God's Word and not just from an older woman's opinion.

When I explained to her about being born again, I told her that someday she would want to ask Jesus to come into her heart and be her Messiah. I marked all the verses that verified His desire for a personal relationship with her. I said, "Someday you may want to read through all these verses one more time, and then you can decide if you would like to pray and ask Jesus to be your Lord and Savior." I offered her this private way of making the choice to receive Jesus, but then added, "Or if you want, we could go outside, get in your car, and you could pray and ask Jesus the Messiah to come into your heart and take control of your life."

Well, this young woman looked at me and said something that really cranked my tractor. Because of her Jewish background and upbringing, she said to me, "Mrs. Kendall, I would like you to witness this covenant." I almost fell over dead. I'm like, "Waiter, check please!" (Of course I left a tip bigger than required because I want to be a good witness, considering that I spent three hours sharing with this girl.) We hurried to her car, and after going over a few verses (so that this was about God's way to heaven and not Mrs. Kendall's advice), I led her in the sinner's prayer. When she finished praying to embrace Christ as Messiah, I gave her the Bible I had marked for her. Suddenly I realized that I was wearing my favorite ring with the Christian symbol of the fish. I immediately pulled the ring off my finger and said, "Daniella, here is a ring that seals the covenant. Ephesians 1:13 tells that when we believe in Jesus as Messiah, the Holy Spirit comes into our heart as the internal engagement ring for the bride of Christ."

My husband called my cell phone just minutes before we were getting ready to pray. He was concerned because I had been gone so long. I whispered, "I'm getting ready to deliver a new spiritual baby." He hung up and prayed for the careful delivery of this new child of God. Talk about being a spiritual surrogate mother!

God's Lunatic

At a conference for NFL players, wives, and families, one woman told me that she committed her life to Jesus because of my life. This woman said to me, "Jackie, if Jesus is willing to walk with a lunatic like you, with all your struggles and weaknesses, then I am confident that He will walk with me, too!"

For some people, being called a "lunatic" would be too insulting to fathom, yet I knew that an approachable God had reached out His hand to Sharon through the weakness of my human flesh. That is probably why God uses people, rather than angels, to communicate the good news...people displaying a reachable God, not reached through being perfect, but reached by trusting in the only Perfect One. Twenty-six other athletes and wives chose to trust in the Perfect One, who used imperfect people to present Him. "But God chose the foolish things of the world to shame the wise; God chose the weak things of the world to shame the strong…so that no one may boast before him" (1 Corinthians 1:27, 29).

Application:
The Stamp of Caring for
Your Children's Friends

Celebrate with the Angels

Last Wednesday, our family had our first "Celebrate with the Angels" party. We placed a porcelain angel at the center of our table, put two candles on each side of the angel, then we lit the candles and served a special dessert by candlelight. Before we ate our dessert, we thanked Ben and Jessica for allowing us to share the love of Jesus with others. We named four people who had invited Jesus to be their Savior and told Ben and Jessica they had a part through their prayers. We reminded Ben about his prayer that one of the ballplayers would be born again and that very night God answered his prayer. We explained we were celebrating with the angels in heaven who rejoice whenever someone is born again (Luke 15:10). Then we prayed and thanked the Lord for allowing us to have a part in the birth of these new believers. After prayer, we ate our dessert. We hope to make the "Celebrate with the Angels" party a cherished tradition in our home every time one of us is involved in the birth of a new believer.

Two Spiritual Birthdays

This month our family will be celebrating two spiritual birthdays, Jessica's on April 9 (5 years old spiritually) and mine April 15 (25 years old spiritually). Both Jessica and I were led into a personal relationship with Jesus when two guys read through a simple gospel tract that explained how to get to heaven. Larry Munos (16 years old) read the Four Spiritual Laws to me at a friend's house, and the good news about God's way to heaven was just too good to resist. A younger man used the same method with Jessica and showed her the only way to heaven. The younger man was her brother, Ben, who was 7 years old at the time.

Sometimes we think sharing Jesus with another person is such a complex journey. Maybe it is for some, but for many, like Jessica and me, someone simply took the time to share God's way to heaven. Larry and Ben read the words and Scriptures contained in the pamphlet and the Holy Spirit did all the rest.

Highway Ministry in Canada

In the summer of 1993, the kids and I and my friend DeDe drove to Montreal, Canada, from West Palm Beach. Caught in heavy traffic on Highway 20 in Montreal, the kids yelled, "Mom, roll your window down, the man in the next car wants to ask you something." The Canadian man had noticed our Florida license tag and wanted to ask a few questions about a family of six moving to West Palm Beach. As our lane inched ahead, I bid him good-bye, and as soon as I rolled the window up Ben said, "Why didn't you give the man a gospel tract?" As the traffic brought him alongside our car again, this time I was ready with a business card and tract in hand. After I answered a few more questions, I handed him the tract and shouted, "God bless you." As we inched away from the man, I was grateful for Ben's nudge to evangelize, even in peak traffic jams. A few minutes later, the Canadian was waving wildly. We rolled our windows down and he shouted, "My name is Jacques, and I too am a born-again Christian." Oh, the smiles on all of our faces as we enjoyed this divine encounter on Highway 20 in Montreal with Jacques.

Velcro Bonding

Gary Smalley refers to the emotional bonding that a family experiences while camping. I would like to add the Velcro bonding effect of driving 3,200 miles with your children in a 4-by-5-foot space. Our summer road trip was like getting strips of Velcro implanted between our hearts emotionally.

As young adults, our children are still repeating to new friends the hilarious stories from their road trip to Canada. May the emotional Velcro from these memories never wear out. Besides Velcro bonding, Moses referred to an activity that parents can do to add to a long car trip "These commandments that I give you today are to be upon your hearts. Impress them on your children. Talk about them when you sit at home and when you walk [drive] along the road" (Deuteronomy 6:6–7).

Introvert at Birth, Extrovert by Rebirth

Two weeks ago, Jessica was sitting near her friend Derek's grandparents watching Ben's soccer practice. I had walked to the car to get something, and on the way back to the field I noticed Jessica was having a lively conversation with Derek's grandparents. I walked up quietly, not wanting to disturb the conversation. As I waited for Jessica to catch a breath, I realized she was telling Derek's grandparents how she had asked Jesus into her heart.

Jessica's liberty to tell adults about receiving Jesus as her personal Lord and Savior began during Spring Training 1992. We had a ballplayer and his family over for dinner, and we were discussing a child's capacity to understand spiritual truth. Ken suddenly asked Jessica to come in from the garage (where the kids were playing) and tell how she was born again. She had never done this before, but she has had no problem doing it since that evening. In fact, this summer on our family mission trip, her testimony was part of the basis for our liberty to lead a teenager on our building team to Jesus.

Our introvert daughter is not shy about sharing Jesus with people. Now as a young adult, she describes herself as "an introvert at birth, but an extrovert by rebirth."

Serving in Africa

As Ken and Ben were serving Jesus on the other side of the world in Mombasa, Africa, I have just returned from a closer mission field—my local gym. I just had the greatest time on the treadmill, sharing the love of God with a Jewish woman named Lori. She told me how she has grown to reject many of her parents' traditions and ultimately her parents' God. She was amazed that I knew so much of the Old Testament and that I had even visited Israel. I can't wait to talk with her again. I am constantly amazed with the opportunities the Lord gives me at the gym to talk with women about the God who wants to be involved in their lives.

On a quick phone call from Africa, Ken was telling me about Ben witnessing to a Muslim woman. As the Rev. Macharia translated, Ken said he was overwhelmed as he watched his son so boldly sharing the good news with this woman. Ken began to cry on the phone as he told me this story, and I wept also. Ken continued to remark, "Our boy is going into the world with the good news." Ken and I have no greater joy than to have a child walking in God's purpose for his life.

Unguarded Flexibility

On a mission trip to Mombasa, Africa, Ken and Ben called, asking for prayer. Their luggage was missing—it was somewhere in Europe. The luggage had been missing for five days. I was really upset for them. Ben said, "It's OK Mom, we are just fine. Remember the song, 'God Is in Control.'" I must admit, I don't know if I would be singing that particular song after five days in the same underwear! The Lord used Ben's response to a challenging situation to remind me of the mature quality of "unguarded flexibility." When they called again, it was to rejoice that their luggage (with all the supplies for the trip) had finally arrived.

As I allow the Lord to mature my character, unguarded flexibility becomes part of a daily lifestyle that I am slowly assimilating.

A Spiritual Baby's Appetite

Last week I had the privilege of leading a 12th grade girl, Lauren, to Jesus. It was especially exciting because I got to deliver this spiritual baby in front of the teenager (Kim) who has been trying to win her to Jesus since school began.

Sunday morning before church, I was standing in the kitchen signing two copies of *A Lunatic on a Limb with Jesus* to give as gifts to my spiritual baby and her dear friend. Jessica asked me what I was doing and I said, "I am getting some food for my new spiritual baby, Lauren." Jessica said, "Would you mind making your natural baby some bacon?" Ken and I burst out laughing at her comment. Jessica brings so much laughter to our lives.

Mentoring and Spiritual Grandchildren

While at a conference in Orlando, I called home to see how everything was going. My mom said she was so glad I had called because our youth pastor had called to give some awesome news. The good news was my spiritual baby Lauren had taken four of her friends to a special youth rally and all four of them prayed to receive Jesus. Mentoring others leads to the birth of spiritual grandchildren. I had the privilege of leading Lauren to Jesus in October, and I have had the joy of watching God use her as a bold witness at her public high school. Her boldness to share with everyone who will listen brings back many memories of my high school experience. She even has the religious background I had and consequently the resulting joy of finding out that she could have a *personal* relationship with Jesus rather than a sterile religious experience. Our teens delivered us to the mission field (youth group) where I had the privilege to lead Lauren to Jesus. When we are involved with our kids, they bring us a mission field.

We didn't just drop our teens at youth group. I am amazed at how faithfully parents will attend their child's sporting event or a musical their child is participating in, yet they rarely consider investing time in the youth group that their children attend.

Witnessing in the 'Hood

When Ben (16) and Jessica (13) returned from their inner city outreach in Baltimore, Maryland, it was such a blessing hearing all the details of the things that God did in and through them. They talked about being in a very difficult situation where they came to the end of themselves and found Jesus sufficient. Ben talked about leading 16 kids in the sinner's prayer, and he was so nervous he almost wet himself. Jessica came home with a heart aching for the children she had worked with. She said, "I didn't want to let them go home; I wanted to bring them home with me." The first day that their van arrived at the inner city location, and after they looked around for a moment, Ben said, "Oh, my goodness—we are in the 'hood." Ben and Jessica spent a week out of their comfort zone where God could intensify their passion for Him and their compassion for others. As I was reflecting on the comments and the pictures of the children Ben and Jessica loved on, I began to dream about a preacher coming out of that backyard Bible club outreach and someday making a difference in the world. Shortly after my time of reflection, I read that Pastor Tony Evans was raised in the very area our teens were trying to impact. Yahoo!

WWJD in Psychology Class

This week in Ben's psychology class, a girl called out from across the room, "Hey Ben, what does your bracelet mean—WWJD?" He said, "The letters stand for 'What Would Jesus Do?'" The girl groaned out loud and said, "Don't tell me you believe in God! My mom has been trying to get me to believe in God for years." The teenage girl began to rattle off a string of protests against the option of believing in God. As she was protesting, Ben said he was thinking of how easily he could blow her away verbally in defense of his faith in God. He said to us at the dinner table, "I paused and considered her harsh voice tone and this thought came to my mind, *Her harshness is a reflection of her wounded heart.* Suddenly I felt so much compassion for her. So when she stopped protesting I simply said, 'I am sorry you don't believe.' And she responded, 'I didn't ask for your sympathy. And you can't make me believe.'" Ben wisely remarked, "You're right, I can't make you believe, I am just sorry you don't." Ben said a silence descended over the whole class—like a holy hush.

As a parent, I was stunned by Ben's sensitivity to the harsh mouth of the wounded girl. I was impressed that Ben's compassion curbed any defensive response. At Ben's age, I was as wounded as that girl, and by God's glorious grace, I did come to believe.

A Witness in the Snow

The day after Christmas, Jessica left on a ski trip with a youth group. This trip was her Christmas gift and we agreed because she was going with so many of her friends from school. We prayed not only for her protection, but also that God would seriously invade this group of teens. When we went to pick Jessica up, we expected her to get off the bus totally drained. Well, she was glowing and when she got in the car, we realized it was a Jesus glow. She talked nonstop for two hours about all that Jesus did on the trip. She and her friends had the privilege to share Jesus with a man in the ski lodge. We just cheered as she told us. I said, "What an awesome moment!" Jessica responded, "That was the highlight of the trip." God also broke a young man that we have been praying about for two years. Jessica cried as she told us what God did in the heart of this young man.

When Jessica returned to school after Christmas break, she was sharing in her Bible class at school what God did. Her teacher said, "Jessica you are glowing so much, you may catch on fire." What a privilege to fan the flame since she got home! My dream, my prayer…children who are blazing torches for Jesus (Isaiah 62:1).

Contagious Christianity

I have been studying a course called Contagious Christianity. The contagious Christian is the person who has caught God's love and contagiously communicates this love to others. Recently, a parent of one of Jessica's friends sent her a card saying:

It must make God so glad to see how you brighten up the world He created. You rejoice in every single blessing He's given you, and you use His gifts to bless others. You spread His love with the smiles and greetings you share with everyone you meet. You enjoy your faith and do God's will with an energy that shows how happy it makes you. God must be glad to have you around—I know I am.

Jessica has been praying for this woman and her husband for a year. Jessica's contagious Christianity is impacting this family, and we are looking forward to what God has in store for them. Jessica is becoming a contagious Christian.

Mary Magdalene of RPB

Because we have a highly verbal home, I get all kinds of details on the young people that my children come across. I remember hearing about a particular girl whom the kids called by a certain name that I can't print—trust me, you would not want your son going anywhere with her, not even church. When I heard about her, I knew in my heart that such a promiscuous child was a likely victim of sexual abuse. I encouraged my kids to pray for the girl.

One day my doorbell rang, and one of my children's friends was at the door with a young girl whom I did not recognize. I invited them to come in, and when Lindsey introduced the stranger to me, it dawned on me that this was the needy girl my children had been discussing. I began to concentrate on her and the young girl said to me, "I heard you wrote a book." I immediately jumped up and ran to get her a copy, and then I signed a special note in it for her. She was stunned by my gesture. After a few more moments together, Lindsey mentioned that they needed to get back to school because they were on their lunch break. I jumped up and hugged Lindsey, and then I turned to hug this wounded young woman who actually held on to me for a moment. When they left, I began to pray for this needy teen.

That evening Lindsey called me and said, "Mrs. Kendall, when we got in the car, _____ said to me, 'I don't remember the last time an adult hugged me.'" No wonder that teen is looking for love in all the wrong places. We know that girls play at sex to get love. That remark brought tears to my eyes. A simple hug of a needy teen reinforced my commitment to the mission field that our children and their friends deliver to my front door.

I want to be the kind of mom that my children know can be trusted with the wounded birds that they bring home, the kind of mom that other children can trust with the wounded birds they are trying to reach out to for Jesus' sake.

Good Girls Need Jesus

Recently Jessica was asked to pray about being on a traveling women's ministry team. As she prayed about joining this team, she expressed her concern that she didn't have a "dynamic testimony" like some of the girls on the team who had had rough lives without Jesus.

This morning Jessica called me, and she was so excited because the Lord had clearly shown her the "testimony" that she has. She said, "Jesus showed me today that good girls need Jesus as much as any bad girl needs Jesus." She said the Lord showed her that she was to tell young women to *come out and be free* in Jesus. "To say to the captives, 'Come out,' and to those in darkness, 'Be free!'" (Isaiah 49:9).

Then Jessica quoted Isaiah 50:4 and said, "This verse is the promise that Jesus will daily equip me with the words to speak boldly to those who are weary in life's dark prison." I had a fit when she read Isaiah 50:4 because that is the exact verse Jesus gave me in 1973 as a frame for the daily ministry I had on my college campus.

Love Leaves a Key Under the Doormat

A couple of weeks ago, one of Ben's high school friends called our home and asked to speak with "Mrs. Kendall." After we caught up on how he was doing in college, I asked him why he had called. He said, "I need to talk to someone I trust about women and God." What was so wonderful about this call was this young man went through a pretty "dark period" in high school. Ken and I decided to "react with extravagant love and acceptance of him" rather than overreact and judge him harshly. After talking for almost an hour and praying for him at the end of the call, fireworks were exploding in my heart. As I shared the conversation with Ken, he said, "Call Ben and tell him who called."

When I told Ben who called and what he wanted, Ben burst into joyous laughter, and then he said: "Mom, this just proves again that you and Dad made good choices as parents in relation to loving my friends unconditionally. When other parents were overreacting and panicking, you and Dad remained steady in loving and praying for my friends, knowing only God changes people. Your unconditional love has kept the door of communication open, and six years later you are hearing from my friend. Mom, you and Dad have left a key under the welcome mat for all my friends. How cool to think when they want to talk about life's most important truths, they are free to call you and Dad."

Questions:
For Individual Reflection
or Group Study

1. What does this quote mean to you as a Christian and a mother: "We love God best when we love each other well"? (1 John 3:16–18)
2. Do you have difficulty loving some of your children's friends? Their friends' parents? (1 Corinthians 8:1*b*; 13)
3. Do you consider it a stretch to embrace less-than-perfect kids as a mission field delivered to your home? (Matthew 5:43–47)
4. How can you apply this quote: "Service is not a gift we give God but a gift that He gives us"? Are you using your gift? (Romans 12:3–8; Ephesians 4:11–13)
5. Make a "God Squad" prayer card comprised of the names of young people who have come into your home who need a deeper relationship with Jesus. (1 Timothy 2:1)

Chapter 7

STAMP THE IMAGE OF
Your Heart's Passion

 **Principle:
Children will catch
your passion for
God and people.**

While standing at the local Christian pub (Starbucks), I read a sign that was posted on the wall. The sign read: "Your Passion Takes You Places." Immediately I thought of another stamp that we as mothers ink up and stamp on our children's souls. This is the stamp of our heart's passion. Where does your passion take you on a daily basis?

Passion has been defined as any powerful emotion or appetite. What is the most powerful appetite in your life? What fills you with boundless enthusiasm? If I interviewed your children, what would they say you are passionate about?

A few years ago, the Lord gave me the most incredible challenge: "Listen for the slightest signal" from my Master. The challenge was based on Psalm 123:2, "We look to the Lord our God for his mercy...as a slave girl watches her mistress for the slightest signal."

God brought to mind an old beeper (no longer active) that I could carry in my purse as a visual reminder to be ready for the *slightest signal from my Master.*

In the movie *Serendipity,* there is a scene where an obituary writer makes a remark about the Greeks not writing obituaries. He says that the only obituary that was recorded when a person died was the answer to one question: *"Did she/he live with passion?"* Regardless of our personalities, talents, or circumstances, we all live with some form of passion for something or someone. Our appetites are obvious to those who are closest to us. Your child mirrors and reflects your passion. The friends you run with also reflect your passion because you tend to attract and hang with people who validate what you think is most important. Recently someone explained that a particular woman got a breast augmentation because all of her closest friends had their breasts enhanced. Talk about running with people who validate your passion about your public image!

When my children were young, I was pretty obsessed about eating healthy. Now, this was before eating healthy became a national movement. I would go out with a certain group of women after Bible study, and they'd tease me the whole time about the way I ate. I used to think, *Well, I'm going to stop going out with that group. I'm sick and tired of getting hassled about the way I eat.* My thoughts reflected my desire to be with people who understood my enthusiasm about healthy eating. We like to be with those who affirm our passion and appetites and do not challenge them.

In the eighth century B.C., an old prophet captured the reality of the relationship between our passion and the friends we choose: "Can two walk together, except they are agreed?" (Amos 3:3 NKJV). The wisest man who ever lived wrote a verse that states that as we associate, we become. "He who walks with the wise grows wise, but a companion of fools suffers harm" (Proverbs 13:20).

Considering that friends not only reflect but also influence your heart's passion, what do your friends reveal about you? What's your passion? What do you have boundless energy for? Does your passion ignite through one of the following: mall therapy, clothes, shoes, model home, more money, popularity, food, body beautiful, hobbies, movies, romance novels, or crafts? Our home, our children, and our friends are all reflectors of our heart's passion. You may think that mall therapy is an innocent female adventure—and at times it is—but too often it is a chance to "feast on the world" in place of feasting on God. "'Everything is permissible for me'— but not everything is beneficial. 'Everything is permissible for me'—but I will not be mastered by anything" (1 Corinthians 6:12). Even chocolate is permissible, but it is not always beneficial, and it is sometimes mastering in its power.

Consider how many women you know who are passionate about their shoes. Their bedroom closet is full of shoes—with not enough days in a month to wear all of them. I know a young woman who can spend seven straight hours at the mall. I remarked about how long she was at the mall and she said, "Oh, my mom and I can spend from dawn to dusk at the mall." Well, the daughter clearly embraced her mother's passion.

A Blazing Torch for Jesus

While reading through the book of Isaiah, I found a "keeper" that stirs me every time I think about it. "For Zion's sake I will not keep silent, for Jerusalem's sake I will not remain quiet, till her righteousness shines out like the dawn, her salvation like a blazing torch" (Isaiah 62:1). My first thought, *I will not stop praying until those whom I love are blazing torches for Jesus.*

The next week I was en route to a big college conference in Austin when I began praying, "Lord, use me to light some torches for Your glory." When the conference leaders gathered to pray, I intended to pray the above desire of my heart, when I found myself praying, "Lord, I want to be a blazing torch for Your glory." Well, after I finished speaking, a college student came up and said, "You were glowing so much when you spoke, I thought to myself, *Her clothes are going to catch on fire.*" Well, you can imagine my typically calm response—I screamed and the college girl stepped back a little. I told her about my prayer and she looked as shocked as I was. Saturday during the invitation, that same student asked God to make her a blazing torch for Jesus at Texas A&M. *Yahoo!*

My precious friend Liz Minnick is passionately committed to teaching young moms how to study the Bible. When her home became an empty nest, she filled it with young moms coming to learn how to study God's Word. The young moms would come with their babies and their portable play pens. The moms would settle their children in their snug resting areas, and then the moms would get out their Bibles and notebooks and learn how to study God's Word in such a way that they were changed forever.

I attended a special birthday celebration for Liz in Austin. Her friends put together a slide show review of her life. Throughout the whole presentation, we saw Liz's passionate commitment to Jesus and His Word and her passion that fueled her noble purpose of teaching women of all ages and stages of life. I cried as I watched the presentation of a 21st century Titus woman.

> Likewise, teach the older women to be reverent in the way they live…then they can train the younger women to love their husbands and children, to be self-controlled and pure, to be busy at home, to be kind, and to be subject to their husbands, so that no one will malign the Word of God. (Titus 2:3–5)

Austin, Texas, is a blessed town because such a noble "Titus" woman lives there and passionately pursues her Lord.

When Passion Becomes Idolatrous

One needs to be careful that her passion does not become idolatrous. What is idolatry in modern terms? An idol has been described as taking the crown off God's head and placing it on a person or a thing. Do you know how you can tell if you've put God's crown on somebody's head? A person wearing God's crown can influence your day—whether it is a good day or a bad day. Only your idols ruin your day. Ouch!

Two summers ago while reading *Spiritual Classics,* I came upon an explanation of idolatry that was most clarifying. A.W. Tozer defined idolatry as "an uncleansed love." He used the familiar story of Abraham being asked in Genesis 22 to offer his son Isaac on an altar of sacrifice. I have always known this as a reflection of the coming offering of Jesus, God's only Son, on the altar of Calvary. But Tozer captured something else in the story that I had never considered. He wrote:

> Abraham was old when Isaac was born, old enough indeed to have been his grandfather, and the *child became at once the delight and idol of his heart.* From the moment he first stooped to take the tiny form awkwardly in his arms, he was an eager *love slave of his son.* God went out of His way to comment on the strength of this affection. And it is not hard to understand. The baby represented everything sacred to his father's heart.... As he watched him grow from boyhood to young manhood, the heart of the old man was knit closer and closer with the life of his son. It was then that *God stepped in to save both father and son from the consequences of an uncleansed love.* (*Spiritual Classics,* edited by Richard Foster and Emilie Griffin, pp. 112–113.)

I never considered the possibility of *uncleansed love* in relation to my children. I never even considered that I was a *love slave* of my children. I never considered that I was more *intoxicated* with my children than I was with God. That day I actually wrote in the margin of the book:

"Lord I want to have a God-intoxicated life. Expose any uncleansed love in my heart." You may be thinking right now that your deep love for your children is absolutely normal. I would probably agree with you. But in the context of your life passion, it is something to consider if you have a shred of *uncleansed love* toward someone or something in your life.

What makes love uncleansed? Simple answer—when it causes me to break the first and greatest commandment. "Love the Lord your God with all your heart and with all your soul and with all your mind. This is the first and greatest commandment" (Matthew 22:37–38). When you love God wholly, you do not have to be concerned that you are not loving your hubby or children appropriately. The appropriate love for hubby and children and friends is expressed in the second greatest commandment. "And the second is like it: Love your neighbor as yourself" (Matthew 22:39). *Neighbor* in Greek refers to close proximity—family, friends, work associates, etc.

All the previous stamps that we have covered were written to encourage a God-intoxicated lifestyle. Where did your passion take you this week?

Just as passion directed your life last week, your passion affected your children also. I read the neatest statement by Luci Swindoll that was a wonderful demonstration of how children reflect the parents' passion. Luci wrote:

> While I was in Africa sharing Christ with the nationals there, my brothers were on two other continents doing the same—Orville in South America and Chuck in Asia. Three siblings who live in

North America were taking love, peace and friendship to opposite sides of the globe at the same time. I was thrilled when I realized that, because our mother taught us as children Jesus's words in Matthew 28:19–20: "Therefore go and make disciples of all nations, baptizing them in the name of the Father and of the Son and of the Holy Spirit, and teaching them to obey everything I have commanded you. And surely I am with you always, to the very end of the age." Here we were, decades later, living out our mother's greatest wish for us in Christ. *Mama can you see me?*

When I read that paragraph, I paused and prayed—again—my own heart's constant cry for our children: "Lord, let our children make a difference in this world for You that is utterly disproportionate to who they are…for Your glory only. Amen!"

Do you see evidence of your passion for Jesus in your children? Or does your passion take you toward investing too much time in what is temporal and not enough time in what is spiritual? Maybe it is time for a little fasting from the world and feasting on God. May the following story put some fuel on the fire of your heart.

Two weeks ago, Jessica gave me a book by David Nasser titled *A Call to Die.* The author had spoken at Liberty, and he rocked the world of many of the students. I was very interested in this book because the students that he impacted are young people who are passionately seeking Jesus. On the front cover is this statement: "A 40-day journey of fasting from the world and feasting on God."

When I saw the verse that opens the first day, it was so common that I almost blindly rushed past it. In fact,

I have memorized the verse, which would precipitate even a rush to the first paragraph under the verse. "Then Jesus said to his disciples, 'If anyone would come after me, he must deny himself and take up his cross and follow me'" (Matthew 16:24).

The Holy Spirit helped me exercise *self-control,* and I took out my Key Word Study Bible and decided to look more closely at the verse before proceeding on the adventure. Oh, the surprise that was waiting for this woman who wants to *fast from the world* and *feast on God!*

Anyone who wants to follow Jesus "must deny himself." When I looked up the word *deny* the room almost began to quake when I read the definition in Greek: "recoiling from, remove from oneself, withdraw from fellowship with, *disown.*" To follow Jesus I *must disown myself:*

- Disown my tendency to be engrossed with my own affairs
- Disown my selfish agendas
- Disown my selfish desires
- Disown my selfish attitudes
- Disown my self-enthrallment
- Disown my self-indulgent schedule

I looked up *self-indulgent* in the dictionary, and do you know what word follows self-indulgent? *Self-inflicted.* An individual harms himself through a self-indulgent lifestyle. Why must I disown myself to follow Jesus? The rest of the verse explains: "he must deny himself and *take up his cross and follow me.*"

My self does not want to pick up a cross. My self wants to avoid the cross. My self-indulgent lifestyle recoils from the cross.

I have so appreciated the reminder to *disown my demanding self* and to actually recoil when I hear my selfish desires screaming for attention. Dietrich Bonhoeffer, who ended his life as a martyr, once said: "When Christ calls a man, He bids him come and die."

I am asking God to clearly reveal to me the areas of my life where I am *feasting on the world rather than feasting on God*. Today I was reminded about disowning my demanding self. "You adulterers! Don't you realize that friendship with this world makes you an enemy of God? I say it again, that *if your aim is to enjoy this world, you can't be a friend of God*" (James 4:4, italics added). "Friend" in that verse comes from *phileo* friendship—to adopt interest with excessive fondness.

Once again my heart is challenged. Do I have any area of my life where I need to "recoil" from an excessive fondness for this world? I am ready with my fork and knife; I want to be feasting at the Lord's table and not feasting at the world's table.

Ready to Feast on God?

In a desire to fast from the world and to feast on God, a very dear friend of mine has chosen a "clothes fast." She is fasting from making any purchases of new clothing. You may grin at this type of fasting, but she knows where her passion takes her, and she is longing to be free of the passion of mall therapy. She wants to be more intoxicated by spending time with Jesus than by spending time at Saks

Fifth Avenue. She has been on this fast for several months, and now her children are being inspired by her fasting from the world's popular drug of choice—the newest fashion. She has inspired me, and I am presently fasting from too many trips to my favorite store—Target!

Recently Jessica and I were speaking at a mother/daughter conference called Yada Yada. During the lunch break, I was looking for Jessica but could not find her. When she finally appeared I said, "Where were you? I know you must be starved!"

Jessica's reply, "Oh Mom, I just spent the last hour showing two Jewish girls verses from the Old Testament that validate that Jesus is the Messiah. I shared everything I knew, and I was surprised how much of the Old Testament I remembered when I was showing them so many different passages of Scripture." Well, I just teared up because I know that Jessica's capacity to use God's Word to present Jesus to a nonbeliever is the result of spending years around people who love and share God's Word…at home, at school, at church, and even in the car riding around with her Bible-banging mom.

At this particular conference, Jessica taught workshops on the importance of spending time in God's Word daily—talk about a child reflecting one's passion. I need to share an amazing aspect of Jessica's passion. Our Jessica is the child who had the harder time with my traveling to teach God's Word. Several times I considered stopping the conference work I was doing because of Jessica's complaints. Her most common remark was, "Mom, I have friends who have moms who love Jesus and love His Word, but they don't have to leave town to serve Jesus and teach others."

Several women said to me, "You better be careful, she may grow up to resent God because you traveled when she was young." (Note: I did one conference a month— and that was too much for our Jessica! I didn't start traveling more than once a month until both our children were in college.) Anyway, Jessica is now in seminary and traveling once a month with me doing Yada Yada conferences. I grin thinking about the life path of ministry that Jessica has chosen. Soon she will be marrying a young man who will be a pastor someday. He will be marrying a young woman who is strong in the Word and absolutely intoxicated with the love of God.

Application:
The Stamp of Passion in
Our Daily Lives

Passionate Parents and a Bride to Be

My husband and I found a card on our bed 44 days before our daughter was married. I share it with permission:

> Dad and Mom,
> I just wanted to say a more formal thank you for absolutely everything! I can hardly believe the wedding is days away. I can't thank you enough for your faithful love, support, and provision.

You both always go over-the-top for me and I want you to know I am a grateful girl. I know there are *no other* parents in the world as giving and passionate as you both are. I hope Drew and I can be just like you guys. You have been and are a beautiful example of putting others before your own needs. I am so thankful for the godly heritage you have handed down to me. I can't wait to grow up to be more like you both! I'll love you forever!

—Jessie

Ecuador Trip

The big grin on Ben's face shows the joy he experienced as a part of a team of teens building a church in Ecuador. A questionnaire Ben filled out for school this week provides a glimpse at the impact of a mission trip in the life of an 11-year-old boy. Ben was asked, "What would be the worst thing that could happen to you?" His response, "For me to be of no use to God." We knew the mission trip to Ecuador would impact Ben's life; we are thrilled concerning the ongoing effect of such a trip not only in Ben's life but in the lives of hundreds who went on trips this summer.

Holy Growth Spurt

Ben has gone through such a growth spurt—two inches in two months and nine inches in three years. As amazing as his physical growth spurt has been, he has also undergone a tremendous "spiritual growth spurt" as a 14-year-old this past summer. The climax for the summer growth spurt was at our church youth camp. Ben, along with 250 campers, spent a week being challenged by one of the nation's most awesome youth speakers. When Ben came home, we couldn't wait to hear all about his time at camp. Here are some of his remarks:

The last night of camp, God moved so powerfully that I ended up on my face weeping in gratitude.... As soon as I can, I want to take EE [Evangelism Explosion] so I can be a better witness for Jesus.... So many of the kids at my school are playing games and do not know Jesus. I want to share Jesus with every one of my classmates this year.

Ken and I have been blown away by the movement of the Holy Spirit in Ben's heart this summer, and we are both concerned that we would continue to disciple Ben for the glory of God. Ken and I are especially sensitive to the reality that this "spiritual growth spurt" has its beginning and end in the grace of God, which was lavished on us in Christ Jesus. Our heart's cry for Ben and Jessica is that they will bring God the pleasure He deserves. We are so grateful for the heritage that Ben and Jessica are from the Lord.

Mombasa or Bust

We asked Ben to write a paragraph concerning his desire to go to Africa. This is what he wrote:

I want to go to Africa because as a Christian I have certain responsibilities and one is to witness. In Matthew 28:19, it says "go and make disciples of all nations" not just here in America. The Lord also said, "The harvest is plentiful but the workers are few." I really feel that God is calling me to go to Africa. I am sure that if He permits me to go that the whole group not just me will reap a plentiful harvest because everyone needs the Lord, especially in Africa during their times of trouble. I just hope, if it is the Lord's will, that I will be able to go and do His will so He may receive the glory. I hope those who read this will pray that God will be glorified through this trip to Mombasa, Africa, and that many will be able to come to know Him as we know Him. Thanks for your time! A Servant of Christ,

—Ben Kendall

Our family heard Scott Wesley Brown in concert (May 1989) and we enjoyed his fun song titled "Please Don't Send Me to Africa!" After that song was sung Ben said, "I'd love to go to Africa." A ten-year-old boy makes a remark that God knew would become a dream and then a mission for a young man. What a blessing to not only be married to a man with a mission, but also be the mother of a son with a mission.

Peer Pressure and Mediocrity

During dinner one night, Ben was telling one of the ballplayers about the "flak" he takes for being excited about Jesus. The ballplayer asked, "Don't you go to a Christian school?" Ben told of several situations where he has been teased by his peers for wanting to share something the Lord has been teaching him. Whenever Ben tries to share something he has read (whether from the Bible or a book by Max Lucado, his favorite author) the guys say, "Save it for Bible, Kendall." When I heard what the teenagers were saying to him, my heart began to cry out for Ben.

As I was praying for a word of encouragement for Ben (and all teens who face the loneliness of being committed Christians), the Lord gave me this thought: *If Ben can stand strong in the face of such apathy and mediocrity, he will be better prepared for the trying times in the future. Mediocrity is harder to face than opposition.*

So many parents fear "peer pressure" in relation to sex and drugs. More frightening to me has been the impact of mediocrity! As far as the quenching of a teen's passion, mediocrity is the most powerful peer pressure.

I pray that Ben and other committed teenagers will learn through these painful teen years that "you can only see a star in the darkness." May we continue to encourage our children to appreciate being stars in the darkness (Daniel 12:3).

Cheerleader for Jesus

Recently I had the privilege of teaching a Spiritual Emphasis week for Kings Academy. After three days of clarifying what it means to have a *personal* relationship with Jesus, I brought 840 pieces of candy to the final assembly in order to celebrate with the students and the angels in heaven—celebrating all the students who made decisions to receive Jesus as their personal Lord and Savior! When I finished speaking, the students presented me with a huge card that was labeled "Jackie Kendall— A Cheerleader for Jesus." With the card the students gave me a Precious Moments figurine of a cheerleader. I was so touched by this gesture because I always wanted to be a cheerleader in high school, but I was not coordinated enough like our Jessica. I had the big mouth for the job, but that was not enough!

While teaching Spiritual Emphasis for the third through sixth graders, I told them the story of Ben leading Jessica to Jesus. I told them about Jessica's struggle to understand what the *key* was to knowing you are going to heaven. What a blessing to be able to use Jessica's personal experience to clarify for so many students the difference between knowing Jesus intellectually and knowing Jesus personally in soul and spirit. Several students told me that the story about the *key* helped them understand and receive Jesus.

Looks vs. Essence

Tonight at the dinner table, we were discussing the girls who were nominated for the homecoming court. Ben mentioned who he thought would be the winner. Jessica and Ken both said that Ben's choice was not the prettiest girl. Ben replied, "I am talking about the calculation of real beauty!" Ken smiled and chuckled and asked Ben to explain this calculation method. Ben said, "A girl gets so many points for the outside beauty, and then she gets points for her inside beauty. The girl with the highest total score is the real beauty!" He went on to explain that some girls have high scores for their outside beauty, but they get negative points for their insides so that the negative points lower the final score in the calculation of real beauty. Well, we all cracked up laughing at Ben's explanation. After laughing, we assured Ben that his calculator was accurate and we are thrilled with his perception.

We are happy that we didn't train our children to *look full* when they were actually *empty*. You can train a child to imitate words and gestures that seem Christian, but passion is the heart's essence. One's essence ultimately is calculated and exposed!

From Siberia to a Women's Stockade

I could never express the overwhelming joy that my heart has concerning the ministry that Jesus has allowed me to have through the book *Lady in Waiting*. I have received letters from as far away as Siberia (from a pastor's wife using this book to teach young ladies in Siberia) about reckless abandon to Jesus. I have been receiving letters during the last two months from the local women's stockade where women in jail have been requesting a copy of *Lady in Waiting*. The letters are very short, but the need is so obvious, and I responded by sending a book and a tract. Amazing how God can take one woman's passion, harnessed in print, and ride it to the far reaches of this world.

A Date with King David

On Valentine's Day, Jessica and eight other "dateless" girls were invited to bring a "date" to a special Valentine dinner hosted by two college seniors who were also dateless on February 14. Each girl was told to bring a very special date—a "date from the Bible." When Jessica and her friends arrived at the dinner, each girl was asked to tell whom she brought as her date. The girls were told before they came that Jesus could not be chosen because He was the ultimate Valentine for each of them. Each girl was asked to explain why she chose her particular date. As Jessica told her dad and me whom each girl brought, I couldn't wait to hear whom Jessica chose. Finally, with the suspense almost knocking me out, Jessica told us who her date was—King David. Then she told us *why*. Jessica said, "I chose King David for two reasons. First because he was a man after God's own heart and second because he messed up royally but was totally redeemed."

Ken and I were so touched not only by Jessica's choice, but also by the precious, godly girls who invested in eight teenage girls on a dateless Valentine night. These college girls are a classic example of single women using their free time wisely. Two dateless college girls inspired teenagers rather than throwing a "pity party" for other dateless girls on their campus.

A Witnessing Car

Recently Jessica's car had to go in for a tune-up. As I was dropping the car off, I glanced at the dashboard. I started smiling as I looked at the Scriptures that were taped on the dashboard, and then I looked at two words that were cut out of a magazine—GOD'S GIRL! I started thinking about the different men in the service department who would drive her car and the simplicity of the witness on Jessica's car dashboard. Then I flashed back to an old Renault I drove during the Jesus movement in the sixties and the Scriptures that were plastered all over the dashboard. I put Scriptures on the dashboard as a conversation piece with the hitchhikers I picked up from time to time. Passion for Jesus from generation to generation—what a privileged legacy. "My Spirit will not leave thee, and neither will these words I have given you. They will be on your lips and on the lips [car dashboards] of your children and your children's children forever. I, the LORD, have spoken" (Isaiah 59:21).

Jesus Freaks: Three Decades Later

I must admit to being a "Jesus Freak." I became a born again Christian during the Jesus movement in southern California. In fact, the Jesus Movement of the sixties, which took California by storm, is alive and well on many college campuses across America today. During the nineties I heard about the "Passion" college movement, but now I have an up close and personal glimpse. Two weeks ago, Jessica called excited about a day of prayer and fasting she and 65 other students were going to be involved in the next day. Students on other college campuses would also be praying and fasting as part of the 268 generation (Isaiah 26:8). She asked if she could read something the students were all going to focus on the next day. As she read this "radical" commitment statement to me, my first thought was, *Wow, the Jesus Movement is alive and well in Birmingham, Alabama!*

The quote opened with the following line: "I am part of the Fellowship of the Unashamed. I have Holy Spirit power. The die has been cast. I have stepped over the line. The decision has been made. I am a disciple of Jesus Christ. I won't look back, let up, slow down, back away, or be still...." As she kept reading I cried silently because the passion in her voice connected with the passion in my soul. I flashed back to my teens when I met Jesus. Although Jessie and I have had two totally different upbringings, the passion is the same. I used to fear when our children were little that they would be immunized against passion by their Christian environment. I feared the second-generation mediocrity that I have seen in so many children. How wrong I was!

Passion is not a reflection of upbringing and environment, but a by-product of intimacy with the Almighty.

Our Passion in Our Front Yard

Last Christmas Ken saw a mini-Christmas story in someone's yard and he knocked on their door to discover where they purchased their nativity scene, wise men, angel, star, etc. When our arrangements began to arrive, I got excited about decorating to bless not impress. Ken began to "assemble" the hundreds of lights on the Christmas display. Our friends began to joke about the *Griswald Christmas* (comedy with Chevy Chase), because of how small our front yard is. When Ken was finished, I smiled and said, "We have the true Christmas story on our lawn."

Scared No More

I got to spend last weekend with our daughter and many of her college friends. Throughout the weekend, different people would refer to Jessica being outgoing and friendly like her mom. Sunday morning Jessica and several of her friends came to hear me speak at a local church near the college. After I finished several of the students said, "Mrs. Kendall, your daughter talks and expresses herself so much like you." After that remark had been made several times, Jessica said, "In the past, I would have been terrified if anyone had compared me to my wild mom. When I was younger, I always wanted to be like my 'calm' dad. But the older I have become, I have become more outgoing like my mom and now that comparison does not scare me!" I have never wanted Jessica to be like me;

believe me, one is enough for this planet. But I have always prayed that she would develop a passion for the Savior. You go, girl!

Questions:
For Individual Reflection
or Group Study

1. If the Greeks were writing your obituary, how would they answer this question: *Did she live with passion?*
2. Where does your passion take you? (Matthew 6:19–21; Luke 12:34)
3. In what way do your friends reflect your passion? (Proverbs 13:20; 27:17; Amos 3:3)
4. Is it possible that an area of "uncleansed love" exists in your life? (Genesis 22)
5. Do you need a little time-out from the world to fast from the world and feast on God?
6. Do you need a fast from mall therapy, the TV, the telephone, your favorite craft or hobby, or something else? (1 Corinthians 6:12–13; James 4:4)
7. How can you already see your passion reflected in one or more of your children? Are you seeing reflections of your passion for things that will last for eternity or things that won't?

Chapter 8

STAMP THE IMAGE OF
a Noble Life Purpose

**Principle:
Being a wife and mother
is a noble life purpose.**

Frederick Buechner said, "A vocation is where your deep gladness meets the world's deep need." A mother has many chances to meet deep needs and encounter deep gladness. Such a vocation is the stamp of a noble life purpose. It's amazing to me how many mothers don't have a clear view of this noble life purpose.

I was asked to speak to a Christian group, wives of professional golfers who were in town for a major tournament, and I asked what topic they would like me to address. The leader said, "The wives need you to address their struggle with what their purpose is in life. They just don't understand their life purpose." My first thought was, *Are they breathing? Do they belong to Jesus? Why don't they know what a noble purpose they have as wives and mothers?* Then I began to wonder if this was a reflection of a generation of young women who have not been taught by older women the noble purpose of a wife and mother as expounded in Proverbs 31 and Titus 2:3-5.

When does a woman's noble life purpose begin? In the 1700s a passionate godly woman, Hildegard of Bingen, wrote about this noble beginning, "You were planted in my heart on the daybreak on the first day of creation."You and I were in God's heart from the first day of creation, because He knew we were going to be the objects of His love and attention. He knew when you were going to arrive on planet earth. He knew His great plan for your life, and He knew the impact you were going to have in your generation. On the back cover of the book *Learning to Be a Woman,* by Kenneth G. Smith, is a key quote about a woman's ultimate purpose:"A woman is not born a woman. Nor does she become one when she marries a man, bears a child and does their dirty linen, not even when she joins a women's movement.A woman becomes a woman when she becomes what God wants her to be."

A Mother's Life Purpose

As a mom, it is so easy to trivialize what you do daily. Of course the world around you does not applaud motherhood as such a noble purpose. God's Word encourages us to not allow the world to "squeeze us into their mold" (Romans 12:2).The enemy of our soul is a master strategist;he wants to minimize the significance of the available, attentive, and loving mother. A mother's love reaches far beyond the boundaries of her house.

Let me give you an example. One mother affected her child's life in ways that, in turn, impacted millions of people in the US. The child's father was an abusive alcoholic, yet in spite of this, his mother constantly repeated a simple phrase over and over again to her son. She would say, "God has a plan for your life. There is purpose and worth to each and every life." This man grew up to be a man "whose soul could be heard in his voice," a man with a personal life goal of "cheering up those he met." And as I recently watched this famous man's funeral on TV, I was captivated in considering the impact of his mother's vision for a noble life purpose. An inscription on the front of the library that was built in his honor reads: "There is purpose and worth to each and every life." President Ronald Reagan's mother planted the seeds of noble purpose in his life.

As a young boy, Ronald Reagan moved all over the US because of his father's abusive lifestyle. However, his mother's steady message of hope influenced him more deeply than his abusive father wounded him. You might not be raising a future president, but you are raising children who can cheer every person they meet with the hope of Jesus. Don't let the world trivialize the noble honor of impacting your children with the hope of a noble life purpose.

John Maxwell expressed this noble purpose when he spoke at my home church this summer:

> I want to make a difference with people making a difference, doing something that makes a difference at a time when it makes a difference.

Parents are so intentional in cheering their children academically and athletically, but they often miss the long-term gift of being the kind of people who influence others by being loving souls. Our love for Jesus affects not only our families but also the people in our neighborhoods and communities. You are not just a mom, but also an ambassador sent to love not only the kids who love your kids, but also the not-so-loving young people. Let me tell you, some of the kids I've impacted the most are the kids who have been the meanest to mine. I've learned to pray and love those kids. I constantly told my children that it was the hurting kids who turned around and hurt other kids, so I encouraged my children to pray rather than join the revenge team.

I jokingly tell people all the time that I hope that I get to live on the street in heaven where Ozzie lives. "Ozzie" is my nickname for one of my favorite spiritual siblings— Oswald Chambers. I have been reading his classic devotional, *My Utmost for His Highest,* for more than three decades. Because I am so acquainted with so much of his heart in print, I am often unaware that I am quoting him. He has a comment about a noble life purpose that is the frame of my life:

> Joy comes from seeing the complete fulfillment of the specific purpose for which I was created and born again, not from successfully doing something of my own choosing.

During the last 30 years as a wife and 25 years as a mom, I have watched too many mothers going after something "of their *own choosing.*" They may get what they want but they lose what they have. I had a friend who was absolutely restless and miserable being "just a mom." She had to get more education to validate who she was. Well, she got more education and a job on a college level. She got what she wanted but lost what she had—she is now divorced and her children have chosen to live with their father. Beware of "something of your own choosing." If God wants you to do something, it will not jeopardize your marriage and children for you to obey Him. I know a woman can get more training and do things outside her home very successfully. The woman in Proverbs 31 was very enterprising and capable of multitasking on many levels, although I honestly believe that all that the P-31 woman did was over a lifetime and not simply one day in her life. I believe that God's script for a noble life purpose has a timing device built in that will not undermine a woman's role as wife and mom.

A Mother's Life Task

Words of Paul the apostle to the elders from Ephesus do a good job of framing a woman's noble life purpose. "However, I consider my life worth nothing to me, if only I may finish the race and complete the task the Lord Jesus has given me—the task of testifying to the gospel of God's grace" (Acts 20:24). I had the privilege of meeting a mom who clearly saw *the task* that God had for her in her hometown. This mother of four girls attended a mother/daughter conference in Austin, Texas. At this Yada Yada Conference, this mother not only received affirmation for her goal of raising godly young girls but she also got a burden for her hometown. As she drove home from the conference she had the thought, *Why can't we bring something good like that to our town?* She knew that her hometown was in dire need of a conference for teen girls and their mothers. This mom knew that a conference that would boldly address moral purity would bring hope to their town where moral impurity was epidemic. Dire poverty in her town had even paved the way for young girls to enter into prostitution to service the military stationed nearby.

This mom returned home with a burden that became a vision for a girls' conference. She was not a trained conference leader, but she was a mom who knew that she had a noble life purpose. She knew that God saved her for a purpose, and she grasped that this purpose was beyond just raising four godly daughters. This mom began to share her burden with *other* moms, and their shared vision grew into an incredible conference. They titled the conference *It's a Girl Thing.*

When I arrived at the conference to speak, these moms had many stories to share with me about all the miracles they experienced as they ventured out to sponsor the conference. A handful of moms yielded to a noble purpose of God's choosing influenced their community and affected eternity. These moms found favor with the school board and were able to use a school facility—no charge. They were led to offer "grant money" so that many of the impoverished teens in their town could attend the conference. Five hundred girls heard messages of hope in music and teaching. I could write chapters on the miracles that the women shared with me. I told the women that the greatest miracle for me was seeing a conference birthed not by professional conference coordinators but by a group of moms living for a purpose beyond themselves. These moms became a blazing torch in a desolate town. This team of moms made God look good. "They are…an honor to Christ" (2 Corinthians 8:23).

So many people think bringing glory to God is some majestic moment in one's life. Wrong! We bring glory to God when we complete each day the work that God intends. There is enough time in each day for the will of God. When I complete my God-given assignment, I have brought God glory. Jesus so simply clarified this "glorifying God mystery" when He said, "I have brought you glory on earth by completing the work you gave me to do" (John 17:4). Did you do what God asked you to do yesterday? If you did, you brought Him glory. Today is another chance to bring Him glory and make Him look good. That is the focus of a life's noble purpose.

I have known a few wives of professional athletes who have grasped a noble life purpose—a purpose beyond their own comfort and abilities. Two wives whose husbands played for the Miami Dolphins decided that they wanted to host a Christmas luncheon and use it as an outreach to the other wives on the team who did not know Jesus personally. They heard about other women on other football teams using their homes as a chance to influence women for Jesus. So these two wives planned a very fancy Christmas luncheon and they invited an inspirational speaker to share the message of hope in Jesus toward the end of the luncheon. These young wives got a glimpse of a noble life purpose that all believers have been given.

Each one of God's children has a designated spot on "His Dream Team." Just think, you're here not by chance, but by God's choosing. His hand formed you and made you the person you are. He compares you to no one else—you are one of a kind. You lack nothing that His grace can't give you. He has allowed you to be here at this time in history *to fulfill His special purpose for this generation.*

> "From one man he made every nation of men, that they should inhabit the whole earth; and he determined the times set for them and the exact places where they should live." (Acts 17:26)

As I travel across the United States speaking, I have met hundreds of moms who are concerned for not only their daughters but also the friends of their daughters. Time and time again, these moms tell me that they bought the book *Lady in Waiting* (about how to wait for God's best and avoid a Bozo). Hundreds of moms, after reading the book, decided to open their home to a study of the book. Their daughters and friends would come and learn principles that will guard their hearts from making a poor choice in the future in relation to a life mate. Some may be professional teachers or Bible study leaders, but most of them were just mothers with a burden for God's best for their daughters and their friends. These moms caught a glimpse of a noble life purpose beyond their cozy homes. I can usually spot one of these moms at every conference I do because she is walking toward me with a beautiful glow on her face. She begins to share her story, and I just smile knowing that this mom has the joy of walking in her life purpose and doing something of God's choosing, not just something she has successfully done of her own choosing.

If you wonder what your noble purpose involves as a Christian, then take a few minutes and read out loud 2 Corinthians 5:17-19. Each of us has an audience that is waiting for us to speak up about our awesome God. Consider taking advantage of where you are and find a chance to reach out and love on women. I challenge you to consider the fact that you are more than just somebody's wife, more than just somebody's mom, more than just somebody's daughter. God is dreaming great dreams and He has a noble purpose for you.

Who would have dreamed that a girl from a totally dysfunctional home could be used by God to write a best-selling book, *Lady in Waiting*—protecting God's girls from a pitiful choice in a life mate? My past could have paralyzed my hope that God would ever be able to use me. Instead of paralysis, I experience liberating hope when I read a verse that would help support the truth of a noble life purpose:

> Who has saved us and called us to a holy life—not because of anything we have done but because of *his own purpose and grace*. This grace was given us in Christ Jesus before the beginning of time. (2 Timothy 1:9, italics added)

That verse gave me such confidence in God's purpose for my life. That noble purpose helped break cycles of generational garbage in my life. You don't have to be like your family; if they are not following Christ they can be a good bad example. That's how I was able to look at it with honor—I'm glad for that good bad example. Now I know what *not* to do. People can either be a good example or a great bad example.

Besides our dysfunctional families of origin, too many women are held hostage to yesterday because of shame. Such shame has a way of strangling their noble life purpose. How often have you heard the shaming comment: "Punishing the children for the sin of fathers to the third and fourth generation of those who hate me" (Exodus 20:5). I can't even count the number of times I was beaten up with that verse before I was studying Exodus myself and came upon the rest of the sentence. The next verse contains great hope, and it slaps tape across the mouth of shame! Here is the following verse: "Punishing the children for the sin of the fathers to the third and fourth generation of those who hate me, *but showing love to a thousand generations of those who love me and keep my commandments*" (Exodus 20:5-6, italics added).

I burst out cheering when I read that. I know that I love Jesus and by His grace I am walking in His commands. I can look with confidence at God's noble purpose for my life because God loves me and I love Him. To walk in one's noble life purpose, one needs daily confidence, hope, and faith, the power of which releases us from that stranglehold of shame.

In the book of 2 Kings, I came upon the story of two desperate lepers who were not only sick but starving. They found a campsite that was deserted but fully stocked with food, livestock, and treasures. As they were enjoying their good fortune, the lepers remarked: "We're not doing right. This is a day of good news and we are keeping it to ourselves. If we wait until daylight, punishment will overtake us. Let's go at once and report this to the royal palace" (2 Kings 7:9).

Two lepers, rejected by society, living daily with bitter circumstances, were capable of thinking about the needs of others. Have you allowed difficult circumstances to keep you from sharing the good news of life eternal in the Son of God?

God used a wonderful book to show me a clearer glimpse of the privilege of walking in my noble life purpose. He showed me that serving Him is the best gift I could ever be given. The book is called *100 Christian Women Who Changed the 20th Century*, by Helen Kooiman Hosier. I would take it to the gym and read it, and I would often end up crying at the gym. One of my favorite quotes from this book is in relation to understanding the joy of a noble life purpose.

> How can you know when the Lord is calling you into some vocation?...You can know by the happiness you feel. If you are glad at the thought that God may be calling you to serve Him and your neighbor, this may well be the best proof of your vocation. *A deep joy is like a compass, which points out the proper direction for your life.* One should follow this, even when one is venturing upon a difficult path.

The young woman who asked this question was guided by this joyful compass and impacted hundreds of thousands of people. That young woman was Agnes G. Bojaxhiu, also known as Mother Teresa.

Carol Kent said, "In comparison to the length of eternity, our time on earth is like a weekend." What am I doing with my weekend? The psalmist wrote, "You have made my life no longer than the width of my hand. My entire lifetime is just a moment to you; at best, each of us is but a breath" (Psalm 39:5 NLT).

After hearing Carol's comment about life being as long as a weekend, I realized that in my 50s I am now on Sunday. As I pondered what I have done with my Friday and Saturday, this thought came to me: A weekend is long enough if each moment is lived within the context of a noble life purpose.

Application:
The Stamp of Noble
Life Purpose

Celebrate with the Angels

During the last week of school, Jessica had the privilege of leading a classmate, Tiffany, to Jesus. As I rejoiced with her, commending her for the courage to share God's simple plan of salvation, I mentioned we needed to have another "Celebrate with the Angels" family time. I asked her what type of dessert she might enjoy during our celebration. Jessica responded, "Mom, would it be OK if we 'Celebrate with the Angels' at Bud's Chicken?" I laughed and assured her we could "Celebrate with the Angels" anywhere!

Mom on Loan

Our children received letters from two Montreal Expos wives. They wanted to express their gratitude to Ben and Jessica for loaning their mom for a week.

I wanted to thank you both for how strong you both were to allow your mother to come here and help so many of the ladies on this team. God used your mother mightily in Montreal, and I know that she might not have come at all if it had not been for your support. I want to encourage you to remain understanding of the miraculous way your parents communicate God's will to men and women…as God's messengers to a confused and frightening world….

—Michele Wetteland

I want to drop you two a note to say THANKS for letting us girls here in Montreal "borrow" your wonderful, wild and crazy mom!!! She not only made us laugh but she truly blessed us with her spiritual wisdom through God's Word. It takes an extra special, really neat family to let their mom take off for one week to be a servant to others rather than just her family, I am so grateful for the sacrifice you made…. Love you oodles!!!

—Amy Sampen

I am so grateful for the support of Ben and Jessica and their awesome dad, who is the ideal "Mr. Mom." Of course, the whole Kendall gang ran smoothly because loving Grandmother Chrest was there to fill in all the cracks left by Mom. I am forever grateful for my mother, who definitely will share in this laborer's reward (1 Corinthians 3:8).

Banana Nerds and Red Licorice

Jessica's class at King's Academy was taking up a collection of various items to send to a missionary family in Japan. Two suggested items captured Jessica's tender heart. The items were banana nerds and red licorice. Jessica came home and pleaded with me to go find these items so she could send them to Japan. As I was leaving for the store, Jessica said, "If you can't find the nerds, please get an extra large package of red licorice." I couldn't find the banana nerds, but I found a large bag of red licorice with a bonus amount. I am so grateful for Jessica's concern for those serving in foreign countries even if her desire involves "banana nerds and red licorice" for the missionary kids. Ninety-two pounds of goodies were delivered to the missionaries by a woman who went there on business and took advantage of the time to do business for the King. (God bless Pam on her next business adventure!)

Tuesday afternoon Jessica was talking about the "ocean food chain" that she was studying for science when Ben remarked, "Our home is like a 'spiritual food chain' with people flowing in and out of our lives, getting the food they need then going their way to give food to others." The three of us got so excited recalling the names of those who have come and gone through the "Kendall food chain."

Appalachia Mission Trip

I just read a quote from the movie "The City of Joy" (about poverty in India) that grabbed my heart. "When faced with people in pain, you can respond in only three ways: you can run from it; you can become a spectator and watch people go through it; or you can commit to the people experiencing the pain and help them go through it." This month, our family will be able to not only see people in pain, but also respond to their suffering. The four of us will be leading a mission trip to an area representing some of the worst poverty in America—Appalachia, USA. In addition to repairing homes, we will be telling people about Jesus Christ, the Repairer of broken lives.

How to Check the Pulse of Your Family

Gary Smalley has written about the secrets of a close-knit family. One of the common elements of this close-knit family is the bonding that takes place when a family goes through harrowing experiences. He uses camping as a classic opportunity for this bonding to take place. To Gary Smalley's camping model, we would like to add the bonding experience of a family mission trip.

Our trip to Appalachia was one of the most meaningful family times our foursome has ever experienced. Our family bonds were strengthened by sharing a challenging situation. A family mission trip is not only a time in which hearts are knit closer together; it is also a time for revealing the family's heartbeat. It is like having a nurse come and check the pulse of your family. I'd like to share what was discovered about the rhythmical throbbing of the Kendall heartbeat:

- Our kids worked harder than we ever dreamed possible.
- Our kids witnessed boldly for Jesus by actions as well as words.

- Our kids prayed freely on the job site as well as in a crowd of kids.
- Our kids worked in horrid conditions and they did not whine. (Mom was the one rebuked for whining!)
- Our family worked together in winning Kim to Jesus.
- Our family was stretched beyond our comfort zone and by God's grace we did not break!

I would like to confess that I was absolutely stunned at the horrid conditions of the job site. Ken had tried to warn me about the poverty in Appalachia, but I couldn't comprehend such conditions in America. But as stunned as I was by the poverty, I was even more stunned with the way Ben and Jessica could work so hard and not complain.

Ben's Support for Africa

What an awesome blessing to see Ben's response to the gifts he has received to help him go to Africa. When people give to bless Ben, the blessing overflows into our hearts. A woman wrote the neatest note to Ben, and I want to note a few excerpts: "I rejoice with you as you follow His voice (not mine, your parents, your peers, etc.) in going to His precious ones in Africa…. I believe in Him via you in Africa. I'm so poor but God is faithful…." She gave out of her poverty and Ben was so blown away that he wrote the following letter back:

I can't put into words how much your gift touched me! I was totally floored to see your generosity in supporting me. I just hope and pray that I will be as willing to serve Christ, as you were willing to freely give of what you have. I often find myself getting overwhelmed by the pressures around me and all I can do to cope with it is to rest in the Lord's unfailing love that He has for me and the rest of His children. The Lord said that He will not disappoint those who trust in Him, so I know the Lord will give you rest no matter what the situation. I can't thank you enough for your support and I will be praying for you. I am very anxious to see what God is going to do in Africa through the team that is going. We would never make it without people like you who are so unselfish and loving. Love in Christ,

—Ben

Ben is halfway to Africa and he is confident in the Provider.

After Ben's Trip to Africa

Ben's first remark when he walked off the plane: "I had such a wonderful time, I want to go on a mission trip for the whole summer next year." I cried and screamed when he said that!

Ben's first story: Boniface the evangelist tried to convince Ben to stay in Africa. Boniface said he would build Ben a house, the school they built could be Ben's church, and Boniface would be his interpreter when Ben preaches. Of course, Ben tried to explain that he was only 14 years old and he must return home to finish school.

Ben's story about his dad: "You guys would have flipped if you had heard dad preaching in an open air campaign (street preaching). You would have cracked up if you heard Dad shouting the truth at the people as they gathered to watch the fiery evangelist!" That was a first for Ben, and I was thrilled because I have seen that fiery preaching side of Ken.

Exciting Statistics, Not Zestless Facts

Listening to the mission trip leader sharing the statistics concerning what the teens did in Ruiz, Mexico, I was absolutely captivated by all that they did: laid foundation for a new church building, ran five different VBS clubs daily, shared the gospel with the Cora Indians (an unreached people group), presented the Jesus film to 750 people, saw 137 professions of faith—all this in only ten days in Ruiz. These statistics were exciting because I knew many of the teens (especially our son) who did this work for Jesus.

As I teared up at the video presentation of the mission trip, suddenly it dawned on me that this trip was only one of 43 trips that World Servants was leading this summer. I sat in church praising Jesus for leading us to work with such an awesome ministry. Ken asked Ben what he enjoyed best about his mission trip to Ruiz. Ben's reply was, "I loved doing Vacation Bible School for the Cora Indians. Crossing a river and climbing a mountain to get to share Jesus was so awesome." The effects of the mission trip continue. A week after returning home, Ben was part of a team of kids that got to do VBS for 200 local kids in a summer Head Start Program. Our youth program so wisely uses the mission trip experience as a springboard for local opportunities to serve. World Servants' slogan is "To love is to serve" and I believe our trips help many learn how to love serving.

The junior high teens from our youth group went to a local Mission-Fuge. The first night Jessica called me, she was so excited that I thought for a moment that the teens had gone to Disney World and not the Mission-Fuge!

She was so perky as she told me about her first day and how awesome it was passing out flyers inviting people to VBS and working all morning cleaning out an old building for this pastor in Riviera Beach. She ended the call by saying, "Oh, Mom, when we were cleaning out this old building, we saw mother-sized rats and it was so cool." I must admit that I would never use the word *cool* when describing cleaning out an old building and encountering "mother-sized rats."

Jessica went on this Mission-Fuge with several friends, but she was placed on a work team for the week with all strangers. When she told me about the team of strangers, I cringed in fear for her, but she quickly said, "It's OK Mom; I am excited about making new friends." These short-term mission projects are wonderful in stretching our children beyond their comfort zones. It seems that God's script for our children is going to inevitably lead them out of their comfort zones into the place where they are acting out His script and not their script.

A Humbling Bulletin Board

When Ken returned from a recent trip to Mexico, he told us about a very humbling moment. A man named Aaron Berman took him into a church in a very poor neighborhood. In the back of the church on a small bulletin board was a picture of our family from an old Christmas card. Ken was surprised and Aaron told Ken that our picture is there to remind the people of the ones that helped Quince de Enero go from a dream to a real church with a little school. Ken teared up as he told us that this little church was the first project he ever worked on with World

Servants, and he had not returned to this particular neighborhood in six years. Mr. Berman said the people always
show the bulletin board to visitors, and they talk about the
people who had a part in building the church and school.
We never get used to the awesome privilege of serving
Jesus and making a difference in this world. Yahoo!

Would You Jump Rope for Jesus?

Looking at pictures from a recent mission trip that Ken
led, I noticed one particular picture. Here is Ken in his
work clothes that included heavy work boots. He was trying to jump rope, and the rope was being turned by two
little kids in the *colonia*. Jumping rope was probably not
something Ken did as he was growing up with three
brothers, so Ken's effort was to be admired. My heart was
once again inspired by the things Ken is willing to do to
take the good news of Jesus to a world outside his comfort zone. This week, Ken and I participated in our
church's missions conference, and we were reminded
again why we serve with World Servants—"One never
has God's heart until one has a heart for the world."

Discipleship in a Lunch Bag

During the first week of school, Jessica decided to look
through her yearbook and find the name of a seventh
grade girl who she knew would be having a nervous first
week in junior high. She bought her the cutest card and
wrote an encouraging letter to her. Jessica said to me,
"Mom, I know how nervous I was as a seventh grader,
and I know how awesome it would have been if an
upperclassman, especially a senior, would have written

a note of encouragement to me." I was so touched by this gesture that I made a commitment to write a note of encouragement to Jessica each week and put it in her lunch bag. As I seek to refresh Jessica's soul, she will have plenty to share with those around her at school.

Jessica showed me a note that her brother had put in her backpack just before she left for her mission trip:

> Dear Jessica: I can't put into words how proud I am of you. You are such a strong warrior! I am so glad that the country of Jamaica is going to have such a shining star for Jesus in it. Always be yourself and the world will have no choice but to change through your witness. I am so proud to be your brother. I LOVE YOU!
>
> —Ben
>
> PS: I am always here for you!!!

Whether slipping the note into a lunch bag, a backpack, or a suitcase, we can always give fresh oxygen to the soul via encouraging words.

God's Script vs. Man's Script

About a month ago, during a special quiet time at the beach with Jesus, the Lord spoke to Jessica and told her that she would be singing for graduation. He even brought to her mind the song she was to sing. When the principal of the school announced who would be singing for graduation, Jessica was not on the program. I told Jessica to cling to what God showed her and to be confident in God's script even if man's is different. Two weeks later, the president of the school was looking over the graduation program and he went to the principal and told her someone was missing. He said that Jessica Kendall needed to do a medley that would include a song of her choice and an excerpt of another song. Jessica and I jumped around praising God that we did not lose confidence in what God had said. God's answer is often later but it is always greater! We couldn't wait to tell the president how specific a part he had in God's script for graduation.

Courage for a Noble Purpose

Jessica has been prayerfully considering a pretty drastic move. She has been praying about leaving her "snug nest" at Samford University where she has so many wonderful friends. She has steadily come to the conclusion that she has one desire, and that is to serve the Lord. She knows that she needs more Bible training for such an assignment. As she struggled with exiting from such a comfy nest, the Lord used a quote by Elisabeth Elliot to quiet her fear. Mrs. Elliot stated that sometimes when you are called to obey, the fear does not subside and you are expected to move by faith against the fear. One must choose to *do it afraid.* When Jessica shared that statement with me, I teared up because Jess has always struggled against fear, and now, whenever she begins to waver about her decision, I just remind her of the phrase that she shared with me: "Do it afraid!"

A Forceful Life

In November 1991, I heard this phrase: "A forceful life, placed by God in a receptive crevice of history." After typing that phrase, the Lord reminded me of one of Ken's favorite Scriptures: "From one man he made every nation of men, that they should inhabit the whole earth; and *he determined the times set for them and the exact places where they should live*" (Acts 17:26, italics added).

More than ever, Ken and I are aware of the "receptive crevice of history" that we have been placed in by God. We want to be faithful no matter what the day may bring. As our favorite writer, Oswald Chambers, would say: "Living a life of faith means never knowing where you are being led. But it does mean loving and knowing the One who is leading."

Questions:
For Individual Reflection
or Group Study

1. What do you consider a noble life purpose? (Acts 20:24)
2. Discuss this quote:"Joy comes from seeing the complete fulfillment of the specific purpose for which I was created and born again, not from successfully doing something of my own choosing."
3. Share what you have done this week, month, or year that you know that you were created and born again to do. (1 Corinthians 10:31)
4. Share something that you have done that was of *your own choosing* that didn't bring as much joy as you anticipated. (Ecclesiastes 4:6; Philippians 4:11–12; 1 Timothy 6:6)

5. Share a dream that you have, and examine it in light of the quote found in question 2. Were you specifically created for this dream or is it something of your own choosing? Is it God's script or yours? (Psalm 139)

6. "In comparison to the length of eternity, our time on earth is like a weekend." What are you doing with your weekend? (Psalm 39:5)

7. "Only one life, 'twill soon be past. Only what's done for Christ will last." How does that truth impact your choices daily?

Chapter 9

STAMP THE IMAGE OF
Teachability

**Principle:
Let God and other
people teach you.**

Mom, resist the urge to take score at halftime. The game is not over yet. Too many moms panic when they see a less-than-desirable quality in their child. Often this quality is a tutorial from the Holy One not only for the child, but also for the mom. During a difficult time as an MOT (Mother of Teen), I wrote the following poem:

*My heart is aching,
The pain is just too deep.
How can I hurt someone
Whom I used to pray over in his sleep?*

How do you hurt the son of your right hand,
The child with whom you have walked so often in
the sand?

How do you break the heart of the one you are
afraid you love too much,
How can you take back the words that are a stinging
touch?

How can you care so much, and somehow be so out
of touch,
With the child you love so much?

So many painful questions running through my soul,
Will he ever forgive me for the mother wounds in his
soul?

Oh how I miss those simpler days,
When trips to the zoo and the science museum were
the craze.

I was a stay-at-home mom all these years,
To be there for you to listen, laugh, and wipe away
your tears.
Oh, how much has changed to think that I am the
one who now causes the
Tears...

—*Mom*

Pretty dramatic poem during my favorite time of year
(Christmas). You may be wondering what had happened

between my son and me. To this day, I have no idea why I wrote this poem. But I remember clearly the stormy teen years with our son. I had such unrealistic expectations in relation to parenting a teenager. I had read books, had attended "Parenting Your Teen" seminars, and had interviewed so many parents I assumed I had the teen thing pretty much figured out. I was naive and, frankly, a foolishly controlling mom.

Our precious son was used by God to remove the scales over my eyes. I had bought into the parenting myth that says all you need to do is follow the correct principles and you are assured of a positive outcome. Ken and I had chosen to break the family cycles that we were raised with and cling to biblical principles for our parenting style.

"Train a child in the way he should go, and when he is old he will not turn from it" (Proverbs 22:6). The word *train* means to dedicate, consecrate, and inaugurate. Well, from the moment we found out we were with child, we dedicated our child to the Lord. We consecrated our children to the Lord. We prayed over them when they went to sleep. We read the Word to them at bedtime. We sang praise music with them constantly. We sent them to a wonderful Christian school. We went to church, Sunday school, church camps, and mission trips. We prayed, laughed, cried, and grew as a family.

When we began to struggle with Ben as a teen, we were quite surprised. In fact, I was caught completely off guard. I cried many a night before the Lord trying to understand what we had done wrong. At a conference I attended, Tony Campolo said, "Parents of good kids take too much credit, and parents of struggling kids take too much blame."

One night I was in the den about 4 A.M., crying about our struggle with Ben, wrestling with God, and wondering, *What more could we have done?* As I kept asking the Lord that question over and over, He led me to read Isaiah 5. When I got to verse 4, I just about screamed out loud. "What more could have been done for my vineyard than I have done for it?"

After reading that verse again, this thought came to my mind, *Now I know how God feels.* That was such a comfort to me—that my heartache with our son was a tutorial. Then the Lord brought another thought to my mind. *In the garden, God had a perfect relationship with Adam and Eve and yet they made a poor choice. Two people living in absolute perfection still made a fatal choice.* So why would I ever be surprised that *anyone* makes a poor choice—whether our son, someone else, or even me? Another thought flowed into my heart that night. Do I judge God for the poor choice that Eve made? No. So why do I judge myself for the choices my child makes?

Ezekiel addressed the fallacy of judging the father for the sins of the children:

> The word of the LORD came to me: "What do you people mean by quoting this proverb about the land of Israel: 'The fathers eat sour grapes and the children's teeth are set on edge'? As surely as I live, declares the Sovereign LORD, you will no longer quote this proverb in Israel. For every living soul belongs to me, the father as well as the son—both alike belong to me. The soul who sins is the one who will die." (Ezekiel 18:1–4)

Now after such a sobering time with Jesus, you would have thought that I would have a deep conviction and peace that passes understanding. I wish that were true, but this controlling mom was still looking for more explanations for the struggle with her teen. I continued to read and search for more answers. God is so patient; He continues to send tutorials to instruct us—*if we are teachable!*

Deputized Nathan

In June of 1996, six months after writing the sad Christmas poem, I was speaking in Houston at a singles conference. While teaching throughout the weekend, I must have made a few references to the struggle I was having with our son. Little did I know that God had "deputized" a modern Nathan (the prophet who confronted King David on his sin with Bathsheba and Uriah) in the audience to speak a strong truth to my heart that day at lunch.

After the conference, the "deputized Nathan" took me to lunch. Her name was Jodi. She was one of the singles leaders and had organized the conference. I figured we would chat about the conference at lunch. Toward the end of lunch Jodi suddenly said to me, "Jackie, may I say something to you?" Because I was "teachable," she felt the freedom to share one of the most soberly painful things I have ever had shared with me as a mom.

Jodi told me, "Jackie, after listening to several references to your son and the struggle you were having, the Lord put it on my heart to tell you one thing: It is not about you; it is about Ben and God. *Not you; Ben and God.*" That phrase shot through my heart like a spear, and

I began to weep. Then Jodi told me her story and it rocked my world. She shared that a mother passionately committed to Jesus Christ raised her and her brother. She was a mother who wanted her children to love Jesus more than she wanted anything else on earth. Jodi said her mother's passion helped drive her and her brother seven states away from her.

Jodi and her brother both moved to Houston. They both turned away from what they knew to be truth and entered the typical single scene. After two years of partying, she and her brother both decided that the single scene was absolutely empty, so they both started looking for a church to attend. They each recommitted their lives to Jesus, and now they love seeing their mom and sharing all the details of what God is doing in their lives. Jodi ended her story repeating the phrase, *"Jackie, it is not about you...it is between Ben and God."*

Before I got home, I called my husband in tears. Ken was on a mission trip and I couldn't wait until he returned home to share what Jodi had the courage to confront me with. When I got home from Texas, I wrote that phrase all over my den where I worked at my computer daily.

Words cannot express how liberating that phrase was— *It is not about you.* Most people are acquainted with the Twelve Step Program for addiction to alcohol, drugs, food, sex, etc. Well, the first step has to do with admitting one's *powerlessness.* Sometimes I think I would like to start a Twelve Step Program for Controlling Moms. (PS: Our son now has a relationship with Jesus that is "white hot.")

Well, that day in June of 1996, I took the first step toward recovering from my own lack of teachability. What was blocking my teachability? It was my propensity to want to control and manage every aspect of the lives of my son and daughter, to ensure success, and to avoid pain in either of their lives. My controlling propensity didn't allow me room in my heart or mind for anything other than "my expectations" for our son. I was so attached to the outcome. I had my expectations bronzed on the mantle of my life. The Lord used Ben to tutor me in the area of tolerance, compassion, and God's sovereignty. I like this anonymous quote: "God has not called us to see through each other, but to see each other through."

Student of My Child

When Jessica was two, a wise woman cautioned me about being impatient with Jessica's shyness. Through this word of caution, I decided I would walk patiently alongside Jessica until her fear turned to courage. When Jessica went to school, God sent two women who were compassionate and understanding about her timidity. These special women, coupled with a consistently compassionate daddy, were used by God to walk patiently alongside Jessica and me.

When Jessica was 12, she spoke 88 lines and sang in front of a packed auditorium—700 people. Everyone who saw Jessica perform the part of Brigitta in *The Sound of Music* remarked about her being a "natural" on stage, so comfortable in front of people. That remark brought many tears to my eyes because I know how God has transformed Jessica's fear into courage. The mother of Jessica's first babysitter said, "If I hadn't come to see Jessica in the play, I would have never believed shy Jessica would speak and sing in front of such a crowd."

In 2000, as a senior in high school, Jessica won the lead in *Beauty and the Beast.* I wept as I saw our introvert daughter glowing as "Belle" in this Disney play. Jessica tells people that she is an introvert by nature but an extrovert through Jesus's power and strength. Ken and I thank God for sending Jane and Pamela into our daughter's life. "Train a child in the way he should go, and when he is old he will not turn from it" (Proverbs 22:6).

To stamp the image of our teachability, we need to be "students" of all those whom God has placed in our lives. Whether it is the tutorial of a husband, an in-law, or a challenging child, being open to being tutored on a daily basis produces a wise woman. All married women have a built-in "tutorial" through their hubbies. The tutoring is intensified through the arrival of children. Additional tutors are the obnoxious, difficult people in our lives. In fact, you may learn more through the obnoxious King Sauls in your life than you will ever learn from a delightful friend.

Some of my hardest life lessons have been through the tutorials of *mean* women. When I saw the advertisement for the *Mean Girls* movie, I just cringed. God has taught me so much through difficult people He has brought my way. I must admit, some of these tutorials I wanted to skip. Because of the tutorials I have had, I see mean people in a different context now. Instead of focusing on the difficult person in my life, I have started to ask myself the question: *What is she revealing in me?* Stop looking at her; instead, focus on what she is revealing in you.

The Lord used mean King Saul to teach me a great tutorial that has me grinning more than whining. I asked the Lord, "Why would you let Saul harangue David and bug him and try to kill him? Why 15 years of this?" Fifteen years of an obnoxious person! What the Lord taught me through Saul and David was that God wanted to make sure that there was not one shred of Saul in David's heart—not a shred of that obnoxiousness. Now every time an obnoxious woman says something cruel, before I jump into a tirade of judging her, the Lord just says, "When was the last time *you* did that to somebody?" Oh! So I'm a student of everybody in my life. I'm a student of my children, a student of my in-laws; I know what I don't want to be and what I want to be. These are good life lessons, so rather than resent them, pay attention and take notes. People will ask, "What are you doing?" and I will answer, "I'm learning! I'm part of a private tutorial of my mentor heart."

If you are carrying a child right now in your womb, or you're a mother of a little one, you must buy *The Key to Your Child's Heart*. It is such a great tutorial tool. My father-in-law read it at age 71, and he wept and said that he wished he had had it 43 years earlier. This book is a tutorial in keeping your child's heart open and teachable. We close our children's hearts off to truth and to hope and to God, and then we're stunned at how they behave. The book shows how parents close their children's hearts, and to close their hearts is to close their spirit. When you are teachable, you can read a book like *Key to Your Child's Heart* and be ready for some adjustments and changes in your parenting style. You may learn that it is not the words you said but the voice tone that cancelled the message you tried to deliver. Keeping your heart open and teachable is the best thing you can do for your children whether young or grown adults.

In *People* magazine, Queen Rania of Jordan was quoted as saying: "I have found that children keep us in check. Their suffering melts away our vanity. Their dreams ensure that we never lose our drive to make ours a better world" (May 2003). This woman was not only a queen but also a mother who was a student of her children. May we all be teachable queens.

A mother cannot be tutored by God and her children unless she understands deep in her heart that God is the ultimate agent of causation—meaning God is the only one who can change a heart. John 17:17 states that God is the one who sanctifies us through truth. In this verse, God is clearly the agent of change. Too many mothers think they are agents of change, assistant sanctifiers. A mother is called to love the child and trust the heavenly agent of ultimate causation with the changing of the child's heart. Some mothers wear "junior-god badges" in an effort to conform the child into their image of a perfect child.

So many women are very concerned about decorating their homes, yet teachability is the most "decorative" thing you can do. "By wisdom a house is built, and through understanding it is established; through knowledge its rooms are filled with rare and beautiful treasures" (Proverbs 24:3-4). Instead of reading only *House Beautiful,* spend time with the ultimate tutoring manual—God's Word.

A Painful Tutorial

I have one more painful tutorial that I must share for the sake of moms who are kept bound by the opinions of other moms. Too often the opinions of others are treated as ultimate truth rather than *just opinions.* Let me explain. For several years, I had a creeping suspicion that our son Ben had attention deficit/hyperactivity disorder, but whenever I would even mention my concerns, the community of Christians that I ran with had one answer for such a thought. "ADHD is just an excuse for rebellion." That remark terrified me and kept me from ever mentioning it again—at least for several years.

While speaking at a conference in Pennsylvania, I had lunch with two educators who both had doctorates in education. They seemed informed and safe, so I decided to mention my concerns about our Ben and ADHD. They gave me the titles of two books to read: *Driven to Distraction* and *No I Am Not Lazy, Crazy or Stupid.* After reading both books, I started to investigate whether our town had a doctor who had experience with ADHD. I discovered that we had a doctor who had worked for 25 years with young people with ADHD, OCD, and other disorders.

I got on a waiting list to see the doctor. When the appointment came, Ben and I both went. I waited in the lobby while the doctor tested Ben. During this interview with Ben, Dr. Miles Cooley asked, "Why have your parents waited so long to have you tested?" Ben's immediate response: "Prejudice." Dr. Cooley told me later that Ben explained to him that his mom's Christian friends felt ADHD was an excuse for restless, distracted kids. In fact, one of my closest friends called it a "rich man's disease" because of the expensive testing. Ironically, during my interview with Dr. Cooley, he asked me a question, "How do you cope with *your* ADHD?" This new information brought clarity not only for Ben but also for his mom. It helped me to understand why I get a little confused at these massive conferences. I speak with so many people, all wanting to talk to me at the same time. My head starts whirling, and as my sister-in-law says, "Jackie, you've got that glazed-over look again." Once again, the tutorial was as much for mom as for the one through whom the tutorial came.

Instead of resenting the tutorial, get excited about all that God will teach you on the new adventure your child is taking you on. Be assured, there are so many moms in your community who will profit from the God-given tutorials that you complete.

> Praise be to the God and Father of our Lord Jesus Christ, the Father of compassion and the God of all comfort, who comforts us in *all* our troubles, so that we can comfort those in *any* trouble with the comfort we ourselves have received from God. (2 Corinthians 1:3–4, italics added)

We are the sum total of all that we have read. In addition to the many tutorials that we experience through our family, friends, and community, there are so many wonderful resources available to subsidize our wisdom. At the end of this book is an extensive list of works that have helped me pass the tutorials God has sent my way.

**Application:
The Stamp of
Teachability**

Student of My Teen

We now have a teenager in our home! Ben turned 13 last week, and his mom shed tears over the years that are gone. No more days of catching snakes, lizards, pygmy goats, or crab spiders or keeping peace on our street as Ben captured the bad guys with plastic weapons. No more trips to the zoo or science museum, which some kids thought we owned because we went weekly, thanks to inexpensive membership cards. One activity that remains as others become memories is the joy of reading and praying each night with Ben.

Teens are a fascinating and crazy group! Having lived with me for 18 years, Ken feels he already has had years of preparation for this special time in Ben's life. At a conference for parents of teens, Kevin Huggins encouraged us to view the teen years as an opportunity to "move into your teen's life with love, grace, and understanding and begin to experience the support, encouragement, and fellowship of a dear and lifelong friend." Ken and I are thrilled about the prospect of Ben and Jessica not only being our beloved children but also precious lifelong friends.

No Instructions with This Kit

Fifteen years ago when they placed Benjamin in my arms, I began to cry. You would assume my tears were from the pure joy of holding our first child, but they were tears of absolute fear. My fearful tears poured out of a deep river of inadequacy that was flowing through my heart as a new mommy. I knew that Ken and I came to parenting with very few skills and so little wisdom. Although Ben and Jessica did not arrive with an "instruction booklet," the Lord has used His manual for life to guide Ken and me step-by-step in this parenting adventure. For years I regretted not coming from a godly home where I could have received a model for parenting. I remember talking to a college professor about my fear of not knowing how to be a godly parent, and I never forgot her remarks: "Jackie, your concern will cause you to lean even more heavily upon the Lord, who can show you how to parent your child."

Recently while rereading *Parenting Adolescents* by Kevin Huggins, I came upon the neatest paragraph that caused me to grin so big I think I got a "charley horse" in my facial cheeks! I realized that not having a system, formula, or model of parenting to rely upon, we had to rely heavily on the Lord. That is an advantage, not a disadvantage!

God seems to refrain from giving these kinds of formulas to parents. In Scripture, He has given broad boundaries for parenting and left a lot of room for the exercise of individual parental judgment and discretion. His plan seems to be for parents to focus on attaining a level of spiritual and relational maturity in which they can start to trust their own parental instincts (which in itself requires a lot of trust in God). *Giving formulas to parents can short-circuit this plan and breed dependence in parents on those who give the formulas (if not on the formulas themselves) instead of on God."* (italics added)

Formulas, systems, and models can all be helpful suggestions, but they can never be a substitute for relying upon God daily for wisdom in this parenting adventure. On Ben's 15th birthday, we told him that we were so grateful to God for the privilege of loving him, and we thanked Ben for being an instrument used by God to help Ken and me grow spiritually and relationally. Ben and Jessica have been used by God to increase our dependence on *Abba* Father.

Mom Learns, Then Jess Learns

Last month Ken and I were able to take a Hawaiian honeymoon to celebrate our 20th anniversary (free plane tickets/free condo). While exploring (Ken's favorite pastime) the island of Maui, Ken started down a horrible bumpy road, and I began to complain and plead with him to get off the road. Ken ignored my whining, and at the end of the road, we found the most beautiful beach/park area, which we ended up visiting every morning. As we walked along this awesome beach, the Lord whispered, "You have found a treasure at the end of a bumpy road!"

This year has been bumpy for Jessica. She has faced several big disappointments and a couple of broken dreams—a lot for her young heart. I told her when we returned from Hawaii that I believed God had a treasure for her at the end of this "bumpy road." Two days later,

Jessica was picked to be a King's Academy cheerleader (something she has desired since she watched her cousins, Kim and Kelly, practice their cheers for King's). Three days later, she was told that her favorite teacher at King's was going to be her personal chaperone for the sixth grade Washington, DC, trip. Jessica was so excited that she said to me, "Mom, something is finally working out for me. This must be the treasure at the end of my bumpy road."

> You let men ride over our heads; we went through fire and water, but you brought us to a place of abundance. (Psalm 66:12)

Another Tutorial from Our Teens

Such irony—in 1990, Ken and I taught at a youth conference in Alabama instructing parents about being "students of their teens." At that time, our children were in second and fourth grade. We were teaching material we had researched and were full of ideas and enthusiasm. Now we are rereading our material so that we can be the "students" our teens need. One of the most deceiving aspects of being the parent of teens is their apparent independence (can dress themselves, feed themselves, do their homework by themselves). We are learning that their "physical competence" does not necessarily parallel their "emotional competence." It is so easy as a parent to take on more responsibilities outside one's home the older our children become, but that is the very place where parents of teens are sometimes misled. I am beginning to believe that the teen years can be as stress-filled as the demanding preschool years. Parents of teens are busier than ever and they are often "too pooped" to meet the emotional and spiritual needs of their teens. In his classic book *Parenting Isn't for Cowards,* James Dobson wrote:

> Parents too often commit every ounce of their energy and every second of their time to the business of *living,* holding nothing in reserve for the *challenge of the century*—parenting their teens. Teenagers are demanding enough for a rested parent, much less an exhausted parent.

Ken and I (especially I) have really struggled lately parenting our teens. I know that we are facing the "challenge of the century" with our precious teens, yet I fear that we are often too tired to handle their needs for emotional accessibility. We are seeking to cut some activities out of our schedules so we can be rested and a little more prepared for the often subtle needs of our teens.

Daughter Teaches Mom

Jan Merritt, a dear friend of ours, drives 45 minutes one way to pick my mother up and bring her to hear my teaching on Tuesday nights. It is such an honor to have my mom present since most of my speaking and teaching engagements are out of town. Every week the Lord allows me to honor and love on my mom in a special way. Hearing her express her joy over something she learned from my teaching is very humbling. One of the women in leadership said I should teach a seminar on "daughters loving their moms." She was impressed with the way I love and enjoy my mother. Well, the other night Jessica called home to share something the Lord was teaching her, and as I was jotting down what she was saying (so I could share it with Ken), the Lord brought the thought to my mind:"Jackie, you get to share and teach your mom each week—'daughter teaches mother.' Because you are teachable, your daughter is free to share and even teach *you* new insights she has gained through searching His Word."

Questions:
For Individual Reflection
or Group Study

1. Read Proverbs 22:6 and share what that verse has meant to you as a mother.
2. What is your reaction to Tony Campolo's comment: "Parents of good kids take too much credit and parents of struggling kids take too much blame."(Ezekiel 18:1-4)
3. Do you have a "deputized Nathan" who can speak boldly into your life? (2 Samuel 12;Hebrews 3:13;10:24)
4. Discuss the truth,"It's not about you," and share about the powerlessness of a mom in relation to changing a child's heart. Remember who the agent of causation is! (John 17:17)
5. Are you a student of your child? Would your children describe you as teachable?
6. Do you willingly attend God's seminary courses presented through your children? (Psalm 127:3; Proverbs 24:3-4)

Chapter 10

STAMP THE IMAGE OF
Your Perseverance

 **Principle:
Perseverance leads to
character and hope.**

On June 4, 1994, my husband and I were seeing the *Phantom of the Opera* at the Kravis Center in West Palm Beach. Just as the lights for the intermission came on, I noticed two ushers heading quickly for our section. When they said to Ken, "Are you Mr. Kendall?" my heart began to race. I knew that something terrible had happened. Let me back up. My brother Johnny did not come home the night before, and my mom called me, concerned. She was so concerned that she wouldn't go with us to see the play. I told her that Johnny would be just fine and tried to encourage her to come with us to the play since we had purchased

a ticket for her as a Mother's Day gift. Johnny had been living with my mom following a horrific divorce and loss of
his job of 17 years.

The ushers took my husband into the lobby, and when
Ken began walking back to our seats, I knew by his facial
expression that something tragic had happened. He simply said, "It is Johnny." He and the ushers hurried me out
of the theater, and when I hit the parking lot, I let out
a scream that should have caused a crack in the concrete
of the parking garage. My brother Johnny had been found
by the police in a hotel—which I had just driven by en
route to seeing the play—and Johnny had killed himself.
Four years previous to this tragedy, my sister Bobbie also
had killed herself.

I kept mumbling to myself, "I cannot walk through
another sibling killing himself. I can't bear our children
having another relative committing suicide." As I was crying, I literally had a thought pass through my heart, "Jackie,
stretch out both your arms. You need an intravenous hook-
up in both arms—an IV of God's grace." I literally saw my
arms stretched out and attached to two bags of God's
grace. "God opposes the proud but gives grace to the humble" (James 4:6). Humble, in this verse, refers to someone
knocked down by circumstances. God's grace places us
back on our feet so we can continue to bear up patiently
under the excruciating circumstances that knocked us
down. Eugene Peterson wrote a book on discipleship
using Friedrich Nietzsche's definition of perseverance as
"long obedience in the same direction."

Where did the stamp of perseverance come in this situation? The two weeks after my brother's suicide were

absolutely incredible. The IV of grace gave me the strength to walk through the unimaginable. Here is a glimpse at grace producing perseverance: During the first week, I arranged all the details of the funeral. I attended an end-of-the-year school assembly where both of our children won awards. After that assembly, the police released a suicide note my brother wrote, and of course, I was the one they gave it to—being the eldest child. The second week began with helping my husband and son get packed for two separate mission trips. Ken was going to the Czech Republic and Ben was going to the Dominican Republic. During this week, the final edit for the *Lady in Waiting Workbook* was also due.

After putting Ken on a plane for Europe, seeing Ben to the train to go to Miami where he would catch his plane, and dropping Jessica off for a youth outreach, I was driving to pay a bill. I think I was in an emotional coma as I drove away, so I didn't see the speeding truck flying through the intersection. I got hit on the driver's side, and as I held on to the steering wheel my first thought was, *Wow, God is going to trust me with a car accident?* The guy in the truck got out and started screaming in Spanish while I climbed out the window on the passenger side and found a phone to call for help. The paramedics suggested I go to the hospital and have my shoulder examined. When my mom picked me up, I asked if we could go by the house and pick up the manuscript I was working on—remember *Lady in Waiting Workbook* was due that week.

So there I was with my mom in the emergency room, and we were reading through the rough draft of the workbook and marking the necessary changes. Now, you may think I was absolutely insane, but I know that unless blood is pouring out of your body somewhere, you wait for *hours* in the emergency room. We sat there for six hours, and actually finished the final proofread of the workbook—right in the emergency room.

They put my left arm in a sling to keep my shoulder still—luckily it was just wrenched. I went home and called my sister-in-law to make sure she could drive me to the conference at Calvary Chapel where I was scheduled to speak the next day. She encouraged me to cancel, considering the context of my brother's suicide and my car accident. I honestly considered it for a moment, but then I noticed in my heart that the two IVs of grace were not empty, and God can be enough.

What produces such perseverance in painful situations? Ironically, perseverance is actually produced through suffering. When a woman perseveres in suffering, character is enhanced and hope is fortified. In fact, persevering in suffering produces an addiction to hope. I am a "hope junkie." This is a biblical reality, not just an experiential conclusion.

> And we rejoice in the hope of the glory of God. Not only so, but we also rejoice in our sufferings, because we know that suffering produces perseverance; perseverance, character; and character, hope. And *hope does not disappoint us*, because God has poured out his love into our hearts by the Holy Spirit, whom he has given us. (Romans 5:2–5, italics added)

Mom, when difficult times come with either your husband or one of your children, do not fear suffering—it just means you are a candidate for persevering hope. You are ready to become a "hope junkie." Furthermore, an additional bonus of perseverance is that perseverance produces character—that means revealing your authentic Christianity. Too many moms spend so much energy trying to escape a trial rather than use that energy to persevere in the trial.

Strength for Perseverance

In his book *Parenting Isn't for Cowards,* James Dobson suggests that parents too often commit every ounce of their energy and every second of their time to the business of living, holding nothing in reserve for the challenge of parenting teenagers.

A teen turns a house upside down—literally. Not only is the typical rebellion of those years extremely stressful, but the chauffeuring, supervising, cooking, and cleaning required to support an adolescent can be exhausting.

If, for example, 80 percent of a woman's available energy in a given day is expended in getting dressed, driving to work doing her job for eight to ten hours, and stopping by the grocery store on the way home, then there is only 20 percent left for everything else—maintenance of the family, cooking meals, cleaning the kitchen, relating to her husband, and all the other personal activities. Now, add to these demands the stress of one or more teens, and life can become overwhelming.

Early this morning a friend sent me this anonymous quote: "Patience is accepting a difficult situation without giving God a deadline to remove it." Perseverance is when people see you doing the same thing day after day and not growing weary. It's long obedience in the same direction. Unbelievers see you loving people who are still rascals. They see you forgiving people who don't deserve forgiveness. Obedience makes every moment precious. Every moment of your life can be precious if, in that moment, you are loving well, forgiving aggressively, and letting God use you to stamp His image on people. You can do that moment by moment.

Somebody asked yesterday, "What do you do when you get tired?" My answer, "Well, that means I am still alive. Being exhausted as a mom is absolutely normal." The most important thing is that I'm always asking Jesus for strength to obey Him, and that is something He loves to give. Do you know how He gives it? The gift of grace that saves us from sin is the same gift of grace that saves us from our own selfish selves daily. That's what grace is about. Everybody thinks grace is the commodity with which we are saved. Good point. Very true. But grace is the strength for me to behave myself when I want to be a brat. When I want to lock myself in my bedroom and eat a big bag of M&M's with peanuts and drink a whole liter of Diet Coke (I never drink my calories). Then, after hours of pouting, I refuse to come out to make dinner! Perseverance allows me to submit to the IV of grace daily so that I don't throw a temper tantrum before my children leave for school or after they come home.

Dr. Tony Evans' daughter was speaking at a conference and she quoted something that her grandma Evans had said many times throughout her dad's childhood. Grandma Evans raised eight children without a lot of help from her husband or anyone else, and many times she would say to her children, "For His name's sake, I stay." The moment I heard that remark, I grabbed my purse and started searching for a pen. I wanted to record it because it reminded me of a little phrase I mumbled to myself when our children were preschoolers. "Up and down, up and down—40 times a day makes me so tired I think I will run away." Of course, I revealed my heart in that whining phrase. How did Mrs. Evans do it? Paul knew how she did it. "Therefore put on the full armor of God, so that when the day of evil comes, you may be able to stand your ground, and after you have done everything, to stand. Stand firm then" (Ephesians 6:13-14).

I heard Kathy Trocolli singing, "Oh God, help me not to run ahead of You or drag behind." I thought about running ahead, and how women do that a lot because we're all so pressured. Aren't we always hurrying our children? "Hurry up, c'mon, c'mon." However, I think that in our pouting, we drag behind. For example, the Lord gives you an idea about something nice you should do for your husband, yet you drag your feet because of some grudge you are nursing in your heart. Or the Lord will give you a nudge about doing something unselfish for a needy friend—but then you talk yourself out of it. How many people are waiting on the other side of your obedience? Perseverance helps us to get going and keep going when we think we have no strength left to walk in that obedience.

The other day I had so much on my plate, and I heard the Lord nudge me and say, "Ask your husband what you could do before he leaves for Minnesota to truly show him how much you love him." I was thinking, Hey, how about him asking me!? Do you ever do this—argue with the Holy Ghost? It seems that I always wrestle for at least a moment, arguing with the umpire of my heart. I know that my obedience can make this moment precious, however, so I went to the den and said, "Sweetheart, can I ask you something?" He said, "Sure." But he was looking at the computer, and one thing I have learned is that if I don't get his eyes, I don't get his ears. Our son Ben taught me this principle when I was a young mother. "Don't talk to a man when you don't have his eyes." I said again, "Sweetie," and he looked at me, and then I said, "Is there something that I could do before you leave for Minnesota on Tuesday that will really make you feel loved?" (Besides the sex thing; that one is obvious.) "Besides that, you know, what else could I do?" He said, "You know, after we finish praying"—we pray together before we go to sleep—"when I turn on my side, if you wouldn't mind for a few minutes, just rub your fingers, just real light, on my back. That so helps me to go to sleep." I said, "Sure, but is there anything else I can do?" And he said, "I'd really like some meat loaf and mashed potatoes tomorrow night." Now, how hard was that? Do you know what the Lord said to me? "Remember, obedience makes each moment precious." The Holy Spirit nudged me to slow down long enough to go the extra mile for my husband.

How many nudges do you get every day? The Holy Spirit nudges you all the time, because the minute you ask Jesus to come in, He comes in through His Spirit, so His Spirit is always nudging, "Hey, hey, hey, turn around and say something to her." "Go over there, she needs some encouragement." "Write so-and-so a note." He's so explicit.

After returning from a women's getaway conference where I taught this message, there was a card from our daughter Jessica waiting for me. I cried when I read it, because it validated what I had taught about a mother stamping the image of perseverance on her children. The printed message on the front of the card stated, "Awards aren't given a nation at a time, a church at a time, or a generation at a time; the crowns are given one at a time. God, Himself, will look you in the eye and bless you with the words 'Well done, good and faithful servant.'"

On the inside of the card Jessica wrote:

Mom, I was sitting here in Lynchburg, missing you, and wishing I could be with you and Dad more often. Anyway, I bought this card, thinking about you, and so I figured I would send it now as your new year of ministry begins. Mom, I only hope that one day I will have as much of an impact as you have had. You and Dad are such a beautiful example of followers of Christ. Thank you for letting me be a little part of your women's ministry. I love you, Mom, with all that I am. I pray for you and Daddy daily and I can't wait to see you, to see what this year holds for us. Love,

—Jessica

Long obedience in the same direction. That's all it's about. It's not a long perfection in the same direction. It's being obedient. I can't tell you how many times I've disobeyed the nudge. But when I obey, there is such unspeakable joy and satisfaction. The enemy of our souls doesn't want us to obey; he is constantly strategizing to block our obedience of those holy nudges. Charles Stanley said, "Satan's tactics do not change because he is fantastically successful at them." The joy of the Lord flows from the specific place of our listening to the umpire. Obedience often requires that we be a warden of ourselves—tending our soul like a shepherd would. "Get back in there and obey the nudge." Sometimes the warden sends me to my room. Have you ever been sent to your room by God? I have. He has nudged me several times saying, "Get out of here now or you will say something you're going to regret." And I say, "Yes, I'm going."

Guess Who Is Coming to Dinner

I learned the coolest thing recently from my newest sister-in-law, DeDe. I was so impressed that I asked her permission to share her story. This story will give you a new way of viewing the trials that will come your way as long as you are breathing on planet earth.

Yesterday as I [DeDe] was driving home, I thought about my husband's week. He had stayed up until 2:00 in the morning for two nights in a row, working on plans for the Coral Springs building department. Now, because of something the owner of the company had neglected to file with the building department, he faced losing the contract after investing so much time and effort into the project. After facing a trial-filled summer, the prospect of yet another difficult assignment seemed like too much to bear. Then the Father gave me a wonderful gift in James 1:2–4 (J.B. Phillips) "When all kinds of trials and temptations crowd into your lives, my brothers, don't resent them as intruders, but welcome them as friends. Realize that they come to test your faith and to produce in you the quality of endurance."

To welcome a trial as a friend—that would mean a time of celebration. When friends come over, you welcome them enthusiastically, you make something special for dinner, and you bring out your best china and crystal. So that is what I did. You can imagine my husband's face as he walked in the front door and here was the table set with the good china and crystal, which is reserved for special occasions. He was definitely wondering what on earth we were celebrating. I told him we had some special friends coming to dinner. It was sweet to see the joy on his face as I shared what I had found in the book of James. I shared that I was going to begin a new journey of celebrating my trials instead of negatively seeing them as intruders. When we fail to celebrate, as I have failed to do many times, we lose our spiritual joy and physically drain our energy. I'm setting the table for my new friend and having a celebration.

Do you need a special occasion to break out your fine china and crystal? Don't wait till Christmas—why not surprise your family with a festive table the next time one of your family members is facing a difficult time? When they see the decorative table, you can surprise them with the "new friend" that will be joining them for dinner.

My husband and I took a man out for lunch after church Sunday to encourage him. We let him share freely about his painful divorce. As we were walking out of the restaurant he said the most humbling thing to Ken and me: "You both are so encouraging because after all these years, you are both still so committed to Jesus and each other—and that example encourages me in the midst of my loss." Remember, perseverance is simply a long obedience in the same direction. Today's obedience will lead to tomorrow's wisdom.

Here is a verse that is an excellent cheer for those who would stop running the race when struggling with perseverance: "For those who use well what they are given, even more will be given and they will have an abundance. But from those who are unfaithful, even what little they have will be taken away" (Matthew 25:29).

Now that verse should give you a second wind for the race you are running! I don't want someone else getting what was designated for me but was taken from me because of my unfaithfulness. Such perseverance requires a "holy intoxication." Thomas Kelly expressed it perfectly: "The God-intoxicated life...nothing else in all the heavens or earth counts so much as His will, His slightest wish, His faintest breathing. And then holy obedience sets in...."

Motherhood requires so much perseverance, and to mentor one's child requires even a deeper measure of this tenacity. Motherhood is the most blessed, demanding assignment on earth. The more I die to my script, my terms, and my rights, the easier it is not only to mentor my children but also to have room to be the wife that my husband has dreamed about. I think Americans are basically overenthralled with themselves, so that the demands of perseverance seem too hard, as if it were an archaic virtue that doesn't fit in the 21st century.

Remember the *stamp of a noble life purpose?* I am convinced that a noble life purpose is sustained and fulfilled through perseverance. Recently, in a new book by Andy Stanley, I found a powerful warning about being sidetracked. In the book *Louder than Words*, Stanley wrote: "Every day of your life you go head-to-head with a master strategist. One who hates you. One who is intent on depleting your character of anything that in any way reflects the nature or fingerprint of your Father in heaven."

How many mothers consider the reality of the presence of such a real foe in their lives—besides maybe a painful relative? Have you given much thought to a master strategist trying to erase the image of God in you? There are probably a million different reasons that a mother would want to just quit. I know two very common strategies used by the master strategist that I would like to warn you about. First, he is the CEO of discouragement. When the CEO of discouragement comes and parks himself in the front room of your heart, perseverance comes to a screeching halt.

Don't Let Mr. D Steal Your Heart

"Why do you discourage the Israelites from going over into the land the Lord has given them?" (Numbers 32:7). The moment I read this verse I wrote in my Bible, "Wholehearted obedience requires one's whole heart and discouragement splits the heart in two." I looked up *discourage* and found two Hebrew words—*lebab*, which refers to courage in the heart, and *nu*, which means to hinder, thwart, forbid, and oppose. So to discourage someone is to hinder courage in their heart. Mr. D comes and opposes the heart of courage and confidence in God. Oswald Chambers wrote: "Faith is unbreakable confidence in the character of God." To be discouraged is to experience a break in your confidence in God's character and power. Discouragement, Mr. D, is broken confidence.

We need to guard against Mr. D's access to our hearts. We must not be casual about discouragement, because a discouraged Christian is vulnerable. Some of the most foolish choices made by God's kids have been during times of discouragement. The enemy of our souls knows that discouragement is a most effective strategy to undermine a Christian's confidence in God. "They discouraged the Israelites from entering the land the Lord had given them. The Lord's anger was aroused" (Numbers 32:9-10).

We not only need to be intentional about keeping discouragement from taking residence in our hearts, but we must also resist discouraging others through faithless comments. We want to encourage (Hebrews 10:24) one another's unbreakable confidence in God's character rather than let Mr. D use our mouths to thwart and oppose the heart of courage. We need to be aware that Mr. D is a relative of Deputy Downer and that they are both employed 24/7 by the enemy of our faith.

This week my younger brother was discouraged by the devastating choice made by a dear friend. I have been so burdened for my brother because I know the oppositional power of discouragement. When he called me, his voice reflected a heart broken in half. I encouraged him to spend some extra time alone with God and the Word. I didn't encourage him to spend extra time in front of the TV or working out or eating his favorite dessert. Unbreakable confidence is only restored through faith, and faith is not on sale this month at Macy's. Faith costs time spent with God in His Word.

Look Out for Deputy Downer

The second strategy that would detour our perseverance is the strategy of "unfair criticism." God used the book

The Stronghold of God by Francis Frangipane to remove some serious cataracts from my eyes in relation to unfair criticism. She wrote:

> A number of years ago, I went through a difficult time in which a handful of people made me the target of ongoing criticism.
>
> There is a type of constructive criticism coming through people who love you which teaches and helps you to prosper; and there is a type of criticism that comes through an embittered spirit that is not meant to correct you, but to *destroy you....*
>
> For three years I sought the Lord, yet He would not vindicate me of their accusations. Instead, He dealt with *me*. He reached deep into the very substructure of my soul and began to touch hidden areas of my life....
>
> The Lord allowed this criticism to continue until it unearthed something deeper and more fundamentally wrong than any of my doctrinal interpretations or sins. It unearthed me. The Holy Spirit began to show me how easily I was manipulated by people's criticisms, and especially how much my sense of peace was governed by the acceptance or rejection of man.

I have known for years that people pleasing is a snare and trap that makes God's kids servants of men and not God (Galatians 1:10). Yet this methodology of Satan still cripples me with such debilitating whispers...until I read the remainder of this page in Francis Frangipane's book:

> As much as I prayed, God would not deliver me from my enemy. He saved me by killing that part of me that was vulnerable to the devil, and He did it with the accusations themselves. I will never forget the day it dawned on me that both God and the devil

wanted me to die, but for different reasons. Satan wanted to destroy me through slander and then drain me with the unceasing activity of explaining "my side" to people. At the same time, God wanted to crucify that part of my soul that was so easily exploited by the devil in the first place!

To inoculate me from the praise of man, He baptized me in the criticism of man until I died to the control of man.

Some of you have not faced unceasing criticism from people, but you have faced the flow of critical whispers within your heart either just before you serve or right after. Whatever the situation, realize that the enemy attacks that part of our heart that is not crucified with Jesus. "I have been crucified with Christ and I no longer live" (Galatians 2:20). Now when I hear the enemy's whispers, I check my position. Am I co-crucified or am I still pacing around at the foot of the cross listening to the enemy's whispers? Then I start shouting the Word back at the accuser! As I quote the Word, I reposition myself by faith as co-crucified. "I have been crucified with Christ and I no longer live, but Christ lives in me. The life [vivid living] I live in the body, I live by faith in the Son of God, who loved [Greek, prized] me, and gave himself for me" (Galatians 2:20).

We cannot allow ourselves to be deterred by the devil's accusation or people's opinions. If the weapon of the accuser is words (whispered or shouted), know also that our victory is God's Word.

When I hear the whispers, I am reminded that it is not about me—so, "Get over yourself, Jackie." That is a modern translation of John 3:30, "He must become greater;

I must become less." How cool to think that God can take something bad, like whispering accusations, and use them to crucify those people-pleasing areas of our lives that continue to resist being nailed to the cross with Jesus.

The best thing I can do for my children and their daddy is to be a mother who understands what it is to die to self and to live unselfishly for Jesus and those He has given me to love daily.

Perseverance in Communication

My husband was away on a mission trip in the Czech Republic when Jessica had returned from a Mission-Fuge trip. She had talked all day about the details of her mission experience. I decided to record in print all her remarks for Ken to read when he returned home. I ended up typing two pages (single spaced). Then Ben arrived from his mission trip, and he shared with me until 1:00 in the morning. When he got up the next morning, he continued to talk. Sunday I took Ben, Jessica, and four of their friends to lunch, and I continued to listen to so many awesome aspects of their mission experiences. When we got home, I was anxious to record all I had heard for Ken. I was getting ready to type all the neat things Ben and Jessica had told me when the Lord showed me the coolest thing: If I had gone to the Czech Republic with Ken, I would have missed all the precious details of their mission experiences.

Teenagers live in the now, and they talk about the present. Let a week, or sometimes just a day, go by and if you ask them how a trip or an event was, their common reply is simply, "Fine." Meaningful sharing happens in the now and not weeks after the event. Teens don't want to repeat themselves—unless it is a funny story!

The Lord showed me that my mom could have been here to feed Ben and Jessica when they returned from their trips. She would even have been willing to clean all the grungy clothes they brought home. But the gift of communicating from their hearts is reserved for Mom and Dad (at least that is the way it is at our house).

I struggled for the longest time about not going with Ken on the mission trip to the Czech Republic, yet this gift from Ben and Jessica has proven to be a matchless experience. Teenagers don't talk when we say, "Well, I've got a few minutes, so what has been happening?" Instead, if they are going to talk about an experience, it will usually follow immediately after the happening! That is why I stay up late waiting for our teens to come home. (I'm a morning person, and I would gladly go to sleep by 11 P.M. and let Ken wait up for the kids.) Waiting up for teens, being home when they arrive from special trips, and just being around when they are around are ways to open the lines of communication that so many parents long to have with their teens. It takes so much time and availability to really hear your teen. It requires not only listening but perseverance.

Application: The Stamp of Perseverance

For the Sake of the Call

Driving to PaPa's condo on Singer Island after our annual Easter egg hunt, I mentioned my need to hurry and change my clothes because I would begin teaching the South America Mission Directors on Easter night. Jessica asked, "How many times do you have to teach the missionaries?" My reply was, "Five nights straight. They are on a tight schedule and this is the only time I can teach them this material." Jessica let out a big sigh and said, "Oh, Mommy, why do you have to do this during spring break when we are staying at PaPa's condo?" The enemy almost stopped me in my tracks through the guilt-ridden thought: I wonder if Jessica will grow up to resent Jesus whom I serve passionately?

I responded, "Jessica, you know that song we love to sing 'For the Sake of the Call' [by Steven Curtis Chapman]? That song expresses why Mommy would spend five nights teaching rather than relaxing in the evening at the condo with Daddy and the kids."

Ken and I discussed my teaching at night during spring break, and we decided that the privilege of challenging and encouraging such godly leaders far outweighed the price tag. I would be with Ben and Jessica during the day, and

Dad would gladly take the night shift. "Therefore, my dear brothers, stand firm. Let nothing move you. Always give yourselves fully to the work of the Lord, because you know that your labor for him is not in vain" (1 Corinthians 15:58).

I am so grateful that nothing we do for Jesus is ever wasted. No drive to speak, no late night counseling, no demanding moment in ministry, no trip that separates us from those we love is ever wasted or lost when they are done "for the sake of the call."

Gentle Rebuke?

Two separate supporters expressed their concern in response to the May prayer letter. They said the Family Corner section seemed to imply that our ministry was more important than our children. They felt we may need to clarify our remarks.

Ken and I have watched people place ministry/work before their children, and that example has caused us to strive for the opposite. By God's grace, I have never worked outside our home. We have driven our kids to and from school (even when bus transportation was available) because we cherish those chats that are often "terribly revealing," especially right after school. We always have at least one parent available (more often *both*) for sports events, school field trips, etc. Ken and I have struggled more with our inclination to put our children before each other than to put our ministry before our children. We attempt to keep our marriage, family, and ministry in proper perspective. We believe perfect balance is not possible—control is a frustrating illusion, especially on this adventure of following a notoriously unpredictable God.

He will have no fear of bad news; his heart is steadfast, trusting in the LORD. (Psalm 112:7)

Be at rest once more, O my soul, for the LORD has been good to you. (Psalm 116:7)

Safe in a Storm

As we prepared for the arrival of Hurricane Andrew, our little foursome felt quite secure within our "plywood-covered fortress." We began to talk about the parallels between the physical hurricane and the spiritual storms that have hit our lives.

We were advised to cover our windows with plywood—like covering our souls with the armor of God daily. We were told to store water in containers and bathtubs—like allowing the Holy Spirit to fill us daily with His living water. We were urged to fill our shelves with readily available food goods—like the Bread of Life, the Word of God that we esteem more than food. Boat owners were warned to tie their boats up in safe harbor—blessed are those who are harnessed to the Rock in life's stormy seas. Through spending time with Jesus, we can do "daily prestorm preps" for life's inevitable hurricanes. "If you falter in times of trouble, how small is your strength!" (Proverbs 24:10).

Jessica photographed our house and the yard so she could mount before and after pictures on a poster that said, "My first hurricane!" This is Jessica's first tropical hurricane, but her first emotional hurricane came when her Aunt Bobbie committed suicide two years ago. She and her brother have been learning about life's delicate balance between "calm and chaos."

Tests of Faith

On August 23, cheers of joy were heard all around our town—and not because the baseball strike was over. The cheers of praise resounded because the report on the biopsy of Ken's prostate came back benign. After Ken arrived home from Africa, he made an appointment with the doctor because he passed a kidney stone on the trip home. (Ouch!)

During a standard physical for a man over 40, they discovered an elevation in his blood test PSA. This blood test is one of the methods used for detecting prostate cancer. Of course we were shocked, and some tears were shed thinking about the possible implications. When the kids returned home from church camp, we called a family conference and told them what we were concerned about and that we wanted them to pray with us.

When Jessica heard about the possibility of Daddy being sick, her only response was to ask two questions: "Is Daddy going to die?" and "Can we all sleep in the same room tonight?" (I bet you can guess what Jessica's love language is—touch/physical closeness.) Ben's response was typical: "This is exactly what we learned about at camp. We are tested so we can decide if we will trust the Lord. This is just a test to prove the kind of faith we have."

We all prayed together, and when we finished praying, we were all hugging when Ben said, "Dad, I also learned at camp that part of trusting God is being free to tell God all your deepest feelings—even feelings of anger." (Ken and I were stunned. *We* want to go to youth camp next year!) When Ken and I went to bed that night, Ken said, "I think Ben has more faith than I do."

This recent test of our faith really showed us again the value of testing. Just as the PSA test revealed a physical condition, likewise the test of our faith reveals a spiritual condition. "These trials will show that your faith is genuine. It is being tested as fire tests and purifies gold—though your faith is far more precious than mere gold. So when your faith remains strong through many trials, it will bring you much praise and glory and honor on the day when Jesus Christ is revealed to the whole world" (1 Peter 1:7 NLT).

Note: Ten years after this story, Ken had kidney problems again, and our family's faith was tested through a fiery trial. Ken had kidney cancer. After his surgery and hospital stay, he returned home from the hospital, and four days later his mother died. The four of us faced another Grand Canyon challenge to our faith. Because of Jesus's grace and strength, we persevered. One of Jessica's friends said, "I have never seen any family go through so many trials." And our Jessica's immediate response was, "If there was any family that could face such trials and still trust Jesus, it would be our family."

Christmases Were Not Always Merry

Christmas 1994 has been recorded in my heart and my journal as the best Christmas I have ever had, except for Christmas 1974 when I married the most wonderful guy in the world (December 21). What made this Christmas so exceptional? For me, it was the "holy moments" when God came so near during our Christmas Eve luncheon and on Christmas Day just prior to opening gifts at Ken's parents' home. During those "holy moments," we as a family sang, did special readings, shared Christmas memories, and prayed together; those were some of the most precious moments I ever remember as a Christian and a Kendall. I used to pray, dream, and fantasize about family get-togethers filled with love and unity. This year my Christmas dream came true, and I may never recover.

One of the things Ken read during one of the "holy moments" was from Max Lucado's wonderful book *God Came Near.*

> It's the season to be jolly because, more than at any other time, we think of Him. More than in any other season, His name is on our lips. For a few precious hours, He is beheld. Christ the Lord. Those who pass the year without seeing Him, suddenly see Him. People who have been accustomed to using His name in vain, pause to use it in praise. Eyes, now free of the blinders of self, marvel at His majesty. All of a sudden He's everywhere. I want to savor the spirit just a bit more. I want to pray that those who beheld Him today will look for Him next August.

Our family allowed God to come nearer than ever before during the Christmas season, and I am already looking forward to His next advent.

Ministry Is Not a 9 to 5 Job

Two weeks ago, I boarded an early flight for a conference in San Antonio. That same day, Ken would be arriving home from a mission trip in the Dominican Republic. That morning I was reading Genesis 31, and the passage put Ken's and my lives in such balanced perspective. In fact, the passage removed any desire to moan or groan about our pace. Jacob was explaining to his father-in-law how hard he had worked for him as a shepherd. "I worked for you through the scorching heat of the day and through cold and sleepless nights" (Genesis 31:40 NLT).

I almost screamed out loud (I was reading on the plane) when I realized that being a shepherd is not a 9 to 5 job. Wow, Ken and I both have shepherding ministries that do not fit into a neat work package. We are constantly reviewing our schedules as we try to allow space to breathe and be refreshed, but some "sleepless cold nights with sheep" cannot be avoided.

Have you ever felt that with the pace in the 21st century, people are busier than ever? Have you considered that Americans are on a unique treadmill? Well, an old friend wrote the most interesting comment in her Christmas letter. She wrote: "Life is rushing by and we are all so busy within our own little worlds…but I suppose life has always been that way. Even my favorite eighteenth-century writers/heroes, Jonathan Swift and Samuel Johnson, complained about their busy, hectic lives in their wonderful correspondence to each other."

As I typed that quote, I just grinned at the reality that the wisest man said, "There is nothing new under the sun" (Ecclesiastes 1:9).

Help us, Lord, to be grateful for the demands of shepherding and resist groaning about our pace. We don't want to be Egyptian-delivered whiners (Philippians 2:14–15).

3³/₄ Inches of Life

While reading my devotions, I found an awesome verse: "You have made my days a mere handbreadth; the span of my years is as nothing before you. Each man's life is but a breath" (Psalm 39:5).

After rereading that verse, I got a piece of paper and I traced my hand. Then I took a ruler and measured the width of my hand. My hand measured 3 3/4 inches. Wow, in comparison to the length of eternity, my 3 3/4 inches seems microscopic. If most of us have only between three and six inches of life, what are we doing with the brief moments that we are here on this planet? That verse was both convicting and comforting. Convicting when considering my daily priorities and comforting when looking at Ken's and my schedule. Our life is often jammed full of ministry opportunities, and now I smile when I think about how Ken and I have been cramming as much as possible into our "3 3/4 inches" of life. A professional baseball player was so inspired by this Scripture that he, too, traced his hand, wrote the verse in the center of the traced hand print, and put the tracing and verse on his locker in the clubhouse.

> Be very careful, then, how you live—not as unwise but as wise, making the most of every opportunity, because the days are evil. (Ephesians 5:15–16)

Committed Climbers

"Now when he saw the crowds, he went up on a mountainside and sat down. His disciples came to him, and he began to teach them" (Matthew 5:1).

The Kendalls have had to climb another high mountain. We have had to climb the mountain of another death of a family member. Seven years ago, Ken's brother Mark died of a heart attack. Now Mark's wife Lee Ann has also died of heart failure. The death of another family member not only brought great pain, but also resurrected so much anger. Why another member of our family? Why would God take both of Kris's parents when he is only 16 years old? Ben asked these hard questions, and God showed us how to respond compassionately to Ben's angry questions. One night when we were talking about Kris's pain, Jessica said, "I almost wish this was happening to me rather than Kris." We were all shocked, and then she explained her remark. She said, "I wish it was me, not that I want Mom or Dad dead, I wish it were me because I know where to go with my pain, but Kris doesn't."

Winston the Widower

While Jessica was on her mission trip, she was asked by the leadership to give a testimony in the Sunday service. She was one of two teenagers chosen to share what was on her heart. One of the things Jessica said was, "God didn't promise us that the Christian life would be easy, but He promised us He would be with us." After the church service, a man named Winston told Jessica that her remarks touched him more deeply than she will ever know. She was a little puzzled because she didn't consider her sharing that profound.

Then, the next day, the pastor told Jessica who Winston was—a father of three young children whose wife had died just two weeks ago. Jessica was so excited when she considered the fact that one remark made by a teenager could help an adult during a very difficult time. Jessica said, "The five deaths we have been through prepared me to relate to Winston's loss." Yahoo!

Ephraim, C. S. Lewis, and Jessica

Joyfully, we put Jessica on a plane heading for Christian camp in Colorado, knowing how much the Lord was going to do in and through her as she served for a month on staff. What an incredible surprise was awaiting Jessica. Of all the staff at this particular camp, there was one woman who was notorious for being so verbally harsh that she often made the volunteers weep. Of course, who was our Jessica placed with? None other than this harsh, verbally abusive woman. Whenever Jess called and told me about another cruel encounter with this woman, my heart broke for her. I kept thinking of the verse: "The human spirit can endure a sick body, but who can bear it if the spirit is crushed?" (Proverbs 18:14 NLT).

When I told Ken and Ben about the verbal abuse Jessica was experiencing, they both became furious and wanted her on the next plane home. We decided that during her next phone call we would tell her that she could come home. The next time Jessica called, I told her that we would gladly change her ticket so she could come home, and her response rocked our world. She said, "Mom, my quiet times have been the best ever, and I am closer to Jesus than ever before because I have to cling to Him every second of the day. Mom, how often does a person get a vote in relation to suffering? How often can a person take a plane ride away from suffering? I know I need to stay and learn through suffering."

Well, this mom started to cry, and I shared with her about my own revelation about being "twice fruitful" through suffering (see the reference to Ephraim's name in Genesis 41:52). I told her that when I became a Christian,

Jesus did not come immediately and rescue me from an abusive father, but Jesus was enough in my circumstances. When I hung up the phone, I was full of such joy. Then I remembered I still had to tell Ben and Ken that Jess was not coming home—knowing that they might not be happy with her decision. The Lord brought to my mind a quote by one of Ben's favorite authors, C. S. Lewis: "When I was a child I chose comfort and safety, but when I became a man I chose suffering." As I told Ken and Ben about Jessica's choice to learn to be fruitful in suffering and C. S. Lewis's quote, they both had peace that she had made a good choice. A decade ago, I wrote about God comforting me through the Hebrew word *Ephraim.* Now Jessica is beginning her journey with Ephraim, learning how to be fruitful in a place of suffering.

Long Obedience

In 1971, my pastor told me that the key to following Jesus was to be a person who could handle the "long haul," which is often hard and sometimes lonely. I am excited about the reality of the fruit of perseverance. Whether we are persevering in our Christian walk, our career, our marriage, our parenting challenges, or good friendships, perseverance has some definite perks.

Recently I told Ken that by God's grace we have stayed married long enough to get it right. We have followed Jesus long enough in the same direction that we have seen many good things brought out of several bad things in our lives. We have been obedient long enough that we are no longer afraid of chaos and lack of predictability. We have persevered long enough to learn how to serve God in so many different situations that have resulted in global fruit as well as local harvest. After three decades of serving Jesus, Ken and I know with absolute confidence that our giftedness in ministry is not our extraordinary talent and wisdom but a steady long-term obedience. The other day a preacher from California reminded me again of the ultimate perseverance verse: "But my life is worth nothing unless I use it for doing the work assigned me by the Lord Jesus—the work of telling others the good news about God's wonderful kindness and love" (Acts 20:24 NLT).

Questions:
For Individual Reflection
or Group Study

1. Share a circumstance that knocked you down when you needed an IV of grace. (James 4:6)
2. Look at the development of an "addiction to hope." (Romans 5:3-5)
3. What does "a long obedience in the same direction" look like in your life at this time? (1 Corinthians 15:58)
4. What are common detours from perseverance in your life? (Ephesians 6:13-14)
5. How do you think selfishness impacts perseverance?
6. Have you been detoured from obedience through either Mr. D or Deputy Downer? (Numbers 32:7-10; John 8:32; Galatians 2:20; Hebrews 3:13; 10:24)

Chapter 11

STAMP THE IMAGE OF
Reckless Abandon to God

 **Principle:
Surrender unlocks
the vault to God's
greatest treasures.**

The tenth stamp could have been the first. This stamp impacts the direction not only of your motherhood, but also of every other aspect of your life: reckless abandon to God. Reckless abandon is terminology penned by Oswald Chambers. Reckless abandon is another fancy English term for surrender. Is your life *totally* surrendered to God? Surrender is what unlocks the vault to God's greatest treasures. Your lack of surrender keeps the vault locked. Do you want to unlock the treasure box? Then surrender!

When *Lady in Waiting* was being edited by Dr. Bill Jones, the question arose, "What should be the first chapter?" When asked what I thought, my immediate response was: "No question, the first chapter needs to be the one on reckless abandon." Why should the topic of reckless abandon be the opening chapter on a book about waiting for God's best in a life mate? If a woman is not where she should be with God, she will pick a loser in 3-D. She will be a "bozo magnet." Reckless abandon to God will cut the line from any potential bozo bait. Being totally abandoned, totally surrendered to Christ will protect a woman's heart from the counterfeit in a journey partner. Such surrender will not only protect from the bozo but may also direct her to a man worth waiting for, such as Boaz. (Boaz is the man who, in the Bible's Book of Ruth, was the husband that God gave Ruth as a reward for her faithfulness.)

A key illustration from the Book of Mark expresses reckless abandon perfectly. After I make a few background comments, we will examine that illustration. When a young woman in first-century Palestine reached the age of availability for marriage, her family purchased a box for her, a box of alabaster if they could afford it, and filled it with precious ointment. The size of the box and the value of the ointment expressed her family's wealth. This box became part of her dowry. When a young man asked for her in marriage, she took the alabaster box and broke it at his feet. This gesture of anointing his feet showed him honor.

Mark 14:3–9 tells of a day when Jesus was eating in the house of Simon the Leper. A woman came in, broke an alabaster box, and poured the valuable ointment on Jesus's head. Luke 7 also refers to this event, and it frankly describes the woman as "a woman who had lived a sinful life" (Luke 7:37). This woman was so grateful for Jesus's forgiveness that she showed her love in an extravagant way that caused onlookers to marvel and talk under their breath. Jesus memorialized her gesture in Mark 14:9.

Costly love demonstrates our love and gratitude to our Savior. Costly love is shown in reckless abandonment to the lordship of Jesus Christ or uncomplaining acceptance when the Lord gives you a difficult assignment. Are you ready to ink up your stamp of reckless abandon to Jesus? Are you ready to break your alabaster box, to surrender even those people and things that are most precious to you? Dwight L. Moody once said, "One life, wholly devoted to God, is of more value to God than a hundred lives simply awakened by God's spirit."

I've been to many rallies where people are excited about God. Their emotions are at an all-time high. They leave the rally, church service, or conference with their tractors cranked for Jesus. Their mouths are full of praise and worship of God. Then they go back home, and as they reenter the "daily-ness" of life, their enthusiasm begins to subside. What was that all about? You wonder, "Hello—where did all the passion go?"

These people had quickened emotions that subsided like the tide going out to sea. If the quickening had been a deeper relationship with Jesus, it would have resulted in sustained devotion to God when the participants returned to the battlefield of life. But they didn't learn about reckless abandon or total surrender.

Does your life stamp on people your lack of surrender, your halfhearted surrender, or your total surrender? Oswald Chambers said, "There are very few crises in life;

the great crisis is the surrender of the will." When you and I surrender, then we have nothing to fear. So many people fear surrender, although ironically, surrender is the safest place on earth. Living in reckless abandon to Jesus is the best way to avoid unnecessary crisis in your life.

Stroking the Face of God

Have you noticed how often a little one will rub or stroke your face when you lift the child up onto your lap? Recently while reading in Zechariah, I came across a most affectionate expression. "The people of Bethel had sent Sharezer and Regem-Melech, together with their men, to *entreat the Lord*" (Zechariah 7:2, italics added).

As I looked up the phrase "entreat the Lord," I came across this phrase in the Heritage Bible. Instead of "seek the Lord" or "entreat the Lord," the translation read "rub the face of God." My heart began to squeal with delight as I thought of the beloved of the Lord sitting between *Abba's* shoulders and stroking His face with our heart's cry. Prayer is a time to stroke the face of our Father.

Francis Frangipane was quoted as having said, "Satan dines on what I have not surrendered to God." Remember that surrender impacts every aspect of our lives. Surrender impacts all our relationships. When I don't live my life totally surrendered to Jesus as my Lord, I will tend to surrender to my own desires and waste my life on things that compete with my intimacy with God.

Living surrendered is living whole in Jesus. He fills the cracks and the crevices that we are tempted to fill by generic things in this world. Leslie Parrot said, "If you try to build intimacy with another person before you have done the hard work of becoming whole on your own in Jesus, then all your relationships become an attempt to complete yourself and it sets you up for failure."

Take a moment and reflect on some past failed relationships. Were you trying to build intimacy with another person before you had secured your wholeness through surrender to Jesus Christ? Of course, a person needs community to grow emotionally and spiritually, but one needs to be aware of a propensity to want people to do for us that which only God can do.

My reckless abandon to Jesus is a continual process. A couple years ago, I was reading and I came upon some verses that challenged me, and I did something pretty radical in response. Here are the verses:

> The LORD said to Moses, "Speak to the Israelites and say to them: 'Throughout the generations to come you are to make tassels on the corners of your garments, with a blue cord on each tassel. You will have these tassels to look at and so you will remember all the commands of the LORD, that you may obey them and not prostitute yourselves by going after the lusts of your own hearts and eyes.'" (Numbers 15:38–39)

After reading those verses and meditating on them all day, I came up with a brainstorm. This brainstorm would be another manifestation of my stamp of the image of reckless abandon. I went to my husband and asked if I could redo my wedding band. I wanted to add a blue cord. So we designed a band of Ceylon sapphires to add to my band of diamonds. Whenever people asked about my redone wedding band, I quoted the verses that inspired it.

A single gal heard my story and went and got her belly button pierced with a blue sapphire. I grinned at her creative expression of her reckless abandon to Jesus.

Boundary on My Reckless Abandon
Recently a good friend gave me an excerpt from Tony Campolo's book *Carpe Diem*.

> I was friends with Ed Bailey right up until he died several years ago. When he was in the hospital after a serious stroke, I went to visit him. In an effort to make small talk, I told about all the places I had just been to speak and how I had come to his bedside right from the airport. He heard me out and then said with a slightly sarcastic manner, "You go all over the world speaking to people who, ten years from now, won't remember your name, and you haven't any time left for the people who really care about you." That simple sentence hit me hard and changed my life. I had tried to learn to set priorities and give my time to those people who are important to me and who really need me. I have decided not to let my time be used up by people to whom I make no difference while I neglect those for whom I am irreplaceable. From time to time I have to remind myself of Ed Bailey's words because too often I let people to whom I mean nothing intrude on the most sacred relationships of my life.
>
> A friend of mine recently got a call from the White House asking him to consult with the President of the United States. He said no because it was to be on a day he had promised to spend with his granddaughter at the seashore. The nation survived without him, the president didn't miss him, and his granddaughter had some precious time with her Pop-Pop. First things really ought to be put first.

Reckless abandon keeps me from wasting my life as a Christian, as a wife, as a mother, and as a friend. Reckless abandon puts a frame of eternity around one's life. In his book *Don't Waste Your Life,* John Piper tells an incredible story of two women who understood reckless abandon:

> In April 2000, Ruby Eliason and Laura Edwards were killed in Cameroon, West Africa. Ruby was over eighty. Single all her life, she poured it out for one great thing: to make Jesus Christ known among the unreached, the poor, and the sick. Laura was a widow, a medical doctor, pushing eighty years old, and serving at Ruby's side in Cameroon. The brakes failed, the car went over a cliff, and they were both killed instantly. I [John Piper] asked my congregation: "Was that a tragedy?" Two lives, driven by one great passion, namely, to be spent in unheralded service to the perishing poor for the glory of Jesus Christ—even two decades after most of their American counterparts had retired to *throw away* their lives on trifles. No, that is not a tragedy. That is a glory. These lives were not wasted.

My stamp of reckless abandon impacted what I did with a free night I had this year. I went on a date with Jesus. When I realized that Ken was going to be out of town and Jessica was going to be busy, I asked myself, *What are you going to do with your free Friday night?* And as soon as I asked myself that question, I clearly heard this answer— *Come away with Me, My beloved.* The Lord reminded me of a single woman I met several years ago who described her elaborate date with Jesus one Friday night. So I decided to go to Ken's parents' condo on Singer Island and spend the evening sitting on the balcony (eight floors up)—waiting for the full moon to rise and enjoying alone time with Jesus.

I brought along my Bible and journal and my prayer roll-a-dex. As I began to pray through some of the many prayer requests, looking out at the ocean, suddenly I saw a rainbow. Now, a rainbow is not unique when it has rained, but it hadn't rained. As I was looking at the rainbow, I started to cry, because I had just begun my date with Jesus, and He blessed me with a rainbow before the full moon had come up! I started to think about what a rainbow represents, and I cried thinking of the many promises that God has made and kept. I timed the rainbow, which remained in front of me for 25 minutes. Part of it actually looked like it was dipping into the ocean. Then I decided to look up all the references to the rainbow in the Bible. I discovered three men who saw three different rainbows, but they all faced something in common—a trying exile:

- Genesis 9:12-17, Noah exiled from all that was familiar through a flood
- Ezekiel 1:25-28, Great Prophet exiled to a ghetto area in Babylon
- Revelation 4:3; 10:1, John, the beloved apostle, exiled to an island in Patmos

As I thought about the rainbows that Ezekiel and John saw, I realized that their view was of heavenly status. Then I realized that the rainbow that we can so casually look at is a reflection of a heavenly prototype, not just a scientific wonder! I will never see a rainbow again without considering "heaven's rainbow of glory about the Holy One."

I began to think about experiencing the beauty of a rainbow without having to go through a storm. Then I realized that we can be rainbows of hope in people's lives even when they aren't facing a storm because they can hear about our storms and see our heart's rainbow of promise. Then when their storm arrives, they will start looking for the rainbow of promise for their heart.

Now as if that weren't enough, as I raised my hands to just praise the Lord for the lesson of the rainbow, suddenly I spotted the full moon. Staring at the beautiful full moon, I thought about how far men ventured to visit the moon and to place an American flag on it. As I pondered the effort, focus, commitment, passion, finances, and sacrifices it took to land on the moon, my heart began to grieve that men would pay such a huge price to touch the moon but are rarely willing to expend such passion to touch the heart of the One who made the moon.

When I consider your heavens, the work of your fingers, the moon and the stars, which you have set in place, *what is man that you are mindful of him?* (Psalm 8:3–4, italics added)

Praise him, sun and moon, praise him, all you shining stars. (Psalm 148:3)

Later that night, as I drove back home from my date with Jesus, I opened my "full moon" roof (sun roof) and was worshipping full throttle. When I raised my right hand through the roof in praise, I started to grin, thinking that at that moment of worship my raised hand touched the heart of the One who made the full moon. Later I found the coolest quote, which reminded me of my date with Jesus. It was by John Maxwell: "When you see a rainbow, remember that one person can make a difference."

Application: The Stamp of Reckless Abandon to God

"Chase Away the Blues" Box

As I was preparing for a mission trip Ken, Ben, and I were taking to Ecuador, I was trying to take the edge off Mom being away—I didn't want Jessica resenting God for her mommy being away again. When she was young, she said to me, "Mommy, my friends' mommies don't have to leave town to serve Jesus, so why do you have to go away?"

The Lord gave Mommy a creative idea that entertained Jessica each day. She was told at the Miami Airport that there was a box hidden behind the couch with a week's worth of surprises for her. The box contained individual gifts she was to open on designated days. Gifts like chalk, stickers, favorite candy, and even a personal letter from brother Ben and "a note a day to chase the blues away" written by Mommy. As Ben and I flew to Ecuador, he said, "I want to be left behind next time so I can have a box of surprises!"

When Jesus took His return trip to heaven, He left behind a "chase away the blues box" for each of us. This box is not behind the couch in our homes, but within the pages of the greatest book ever written—God's Word. The box is full of promises that only our disobedience can keep us from accessing.

Life Is So Unnerving

Jessica was waltzing around the family room, singing a tune from the movie *Beauty and the Beast.* I asked her what she was singing (she had been repeating the line several times). She said, "Life is so unnerving for a servant who's not serving." I asked her who sang that song in the movie and she said, "Lumiere, the candlestick in the castle where the Beast lived."

As Jessica continued to dance around the family room, gliding across the tile, repeating the same phrase, a light went on in my head. I thought of how unnerving life is for the Christian who is not freely serving the Lord. Suddenly the singing candlestick's line seemed a challenge for the New Year. With the beginning of a New Year, each of us is given 525,600 minutes to use as we freely choose. May we be careful how we use our half a million minutes each year. I considered what I did with the minutes I was given in 1994. Was life sometimes so unnerving because I was not freely serving?

Christmas Memories

During this year, Jessica read *The Hiding Place* by Corrie ten Boom, and recently we read it again out loud (her request). A couple weeks ago, we rented the movie based on the book and watched it one Sunday afternoon. I found an old copy of *Corrie's Christmas Memories,* and Jessica wanted me to read it to her. Since it was a Christmas book, we were both anxious to read it. Christmas is our favorite time of year, and Jessica and I stretch this Christmas season as far as we can without driving Ken and Ben crazy! In fact, the Christmas season begins officially for Jessica and me the day after Thanksgiving! I am so grateful for Jessica because she brings the joy, music, and laughter to this wonderful time of year. Jessica keeps us constantly aware of the preciousness of this time of year. Without her, the three of us might rush right through this special holiday season. Jessica squeals in delight when she hears a Christmas song or sees another house with Christmas lights. The joy she brings has been used by God to heal some hurts that my heart received during some Christmases past. Jessica keeps "Scrooge" away from our home during the holidays.

One night while reading from *Corrie's Christmas Memories,* I read a very painful story from Christmas 1944 when Corrie was still in the prison camp at Ravensbruck. The story overwhelmed me; here is an excerpt:

> It was Christmas, 1944, and Betsie had died. I was in a hospital barracks in Ravensbruck. There were Christmas trees in the street between the barracks. Why, I don't know. They were the saddest Christmas trees I ever saw in my life. I am sure it was with the purpose of blaspheming that they had thrown dead bodies of prisoners under the Christmas trees.

The story continues with Corrie telling how she shared the love of God with a young woman in the hospital ward with her. She spoke lovingly about the Christ of Christmas; her horrible circumstances with those saddest of Christmas trees did not keep her from sharing the love of Jesus with those around her.

A Hallmark Winner

Ken was on a mission trip in the Dominican Republic on his birthday. When he returned from his trip, the kids had a gift and cards for him. I arrived home two days later, and Ken asked me if I had seen the card that Jessica had made for him. Yes, I had seen it and it had touched my heart as deeply as it had touched his.

She wrote, "Dad, I missed you a lot while you were gone. I hope you had a great trip and a fabulous birthday. I wish you could have been home with us, though. But I know you were out in the world making a difference for people's eternity—so I guess it's acceptable—just kidding! I love you more and more every day."

Diluted Passion

One of the most painful things I have ever experienced as a Christian is watching someone I love roam away from the Lord. During the last 32 years, I have seen many Christians allow their life circumstances to dilute the passion they have for Jesus. As Christian marriages are torn asunder and teens turn away from the truths of their childhood, the ache in my soul sometimes feels unbearable. After many tears, prayer, and fasting, the Lord answered my broken heart concerning the diluting of passion in the lives of so many I know and love. He allowed my brother in Christ Brennan Manning to speak volumes to my broken heart:

The Lion of Judah in His present risenness pursues, tracks, and stalks us here and now. When we cry out with Jeremiah, "Enough already! Leave me alone in my melancholy," the Shepherd replies, "I will not leave you alone. You are mine. I know each of my sheep by name. You belong to me. If you think I am finished with you, if you think I am a small god that you can keep a safe distance, I will pounce upon you like a roaring lion, tear you to pieces, rip you to shreds, and break every bone in your body. *Then I will mend you, cradle you in my arms, and kiss you tenderly...."*

My peace today is that the Lion of Judah will never leave those I love alone. The start is the promise of the completion. Yahoo!

Treasure Hunt Dad

Recently while cleaning out two large filing cabinets, I came across a folder that was labeled "Dad's Treasure Hunt." As I examined the contents of the file, I started to cry as I read the typed details of a treasure hunt Ken had prepared for our children. They were so precious, as was the time Ken took to think it up and type it out.

That very evening, when Ken came home from work, I saw him carrying a bag from Hallmark. I assumed he had bought a Father's Day card for his dad, but I was wrong. Ken pulled out two of the most incredible cards, one honoring a son and one honoring a daughter. I asked Ken, "What is the occasion?" He said, "I went to Hallmark to buy you a little gift, and while I was there I started thinking about there being a Mother's Day and Father's Day but what about a Kid's Day? So I decided I wanted to

buy the cards to tell them how much I appreciate them."
In one day, here were two incidences that verified my
feelings of the last 22 years—I believe Ben and Jessica
Kendall have been blessed with the most awesome
earthly father! I used to dream about an "ideal father"
when I was a young girl, and it came true for our
children. Reckless abandon kept a girl from a very
dysfunctional home from marrying a bozo!

A Most Revealing Picture

When Jessica was transferring to a new college (Liberty
University), Ken and I wanted to help her move all her
stuff to Lynchburg, Virginia. She had a lot of stuff to move
up to the third floor of the apartment complex. After
much "holy sweat," she was finally moved in. Before we
left for home, I took pictures of her apartment. When
I picked up the developed pictures, I came upon a picture of her bedroom that brought tears to my eyes. What
caused my tears were certain objects in the picture:
a beautiful cross above her bed, an alabaster jar on her
nightstand (a symbol from the first chapter of *Lady in
Waiting*—"Lady of Reckless Abandon"), and, on her bed,
her Hebrew-Greek Word Study Bible, her journal, and her
prayer promise cloth. All these objects reminded me why
we could leave Jessica and drive home to Florida with
absolute peace. She has a single-minded devotion to God,
and we are thrilled she is going to get more intensive
Bible training.

Questions:
For Individual Reflection
or Group Study

1. Discuss reckless abandon in relation to the alabaster jar. (Mark 14:3-9; Luke 7:36-48)

2. Discuss the quote by Dwight L. Moody: "One life, wholly devoted to God, is of more value to God than a hundred lives simply awakened by God's spirit." (Acts 17:28; 1 Corinthians 2:2; Philippians 1:21)

3. Describe a time when you were deeply challenged to surrender to Jesus.

4. If the only crisis is ultimately surrender, what keeps us as moms from surrendering our alabaster jars to Jesus?

5. "If you try to build intimacy with another person before you have done the hard work of becoming whole on your own in Jesus, then all your relationships become an attempt to complete yourself and it sets you up for failure." What blocks you from becoming whole on your own in Jesus? (Hebrews 12:1)

6. Do you ever feel frustrated about "wasting your life"? Explain. What has helped you use your time more wisely—with more of an eternal viewpoint?

Chapter 12

STAMP THE IMAGE OF
an Adapting Spouse

 **Principle:
A good marriage
is comprised of
two good forgivers.**

L ast, but not least, is the stamp of the image of an *adapting* (I'm choosing to use that word rather than submissive) spouse. *Submission* is almost like a curse word among women in the United States. I am not trying to be politically correct by using the term *adapting* rather than *submissive*. Adapting is what both husband and wife must do to remain married for more than a weekend. The Word of God calls for mutual submission before it calls for wives to submit to their husbands. "Submit to one another out of reverence for Christ. Wives, submit to your husbands as to the Lord" (Ephesians 5:21–22). We wives are

247

instructed to adapt to our own husbands. I have been adapting to my husband for 30 years.

The stamp of the image of an adapting spouse is a stamp of an individual who has learned something about living unselfishly. A wife's ability to adapt to her husband is a reflection of her own level of selflessness. You may be wondering where I got the word *adapt*. I found it while studying Genesis 2:18, "The LORD God said, 'It is not good for the man to be alone. I will make a helper *suitable* for him'" (italics added).

When people discuss this verse, they always focus on the word *helper*. I was drawn instead to the adjective describing the type of helper, a *suitable* helper. What is a suitable helper? In the Hebrew lexical aid, *suitable* is described as "one like but facing the opposite." Being a helper to your husband means that he is facing someone like him but opposite.

Many people are so afraid of the opposite, but the opposite is God's brilliant intention. Do you know what the point is of *one like but facing the opposite*? A man got in my face one day after Sunday school and said to me, "Why in the world would God make us so opposite and then ask us to love each other and live together for more than two days?" When he was finished ranting, I asked him, "Are you about done?" He actually calmly replied, "Yes."

Then I said to him, "Do you know why God made us opposites? God made us opposite of one another in order to teach us to live unselfishly. The only way you can live with the opposite sex on a long-term basis is to learn how to live unselfishly." Now the man looked like he had been struck by lightning. He said, "Wow, I had no idea." And to be honest, I had never even thought about that question until the moment the man started ranting about it.

Do you know what self-control is? I wear a bracelet engraved with the fruits of the Spirit as a reminder of the life the Spirit wants to develop in me. One of the fruits of the Spirit is self-control. I looked up self-control, and in the Greek lexicon, it is defined as "voluntary limitation of my freedom." Selfishness would assault the notion of my having to limit my freedom for my husband. Why do *I* have to say, "I'm sorry," first? Why do *I* have to worry about what makes him feel loved? Why do *I* have to sleep with the air-conditioning set on arctic freeze?

It takes a lifetime to learn how to best adapt to your husband. We're all perpetual learners. A statement written by our daughter on our 28th anniversary card is very revealing about Ken and me learning how to adapt to each other—since we are one of the world's most opposite couples. Our daughter is our more critical child, so when I realized she was personally writing our anniversary card, I was kind of scared to read it. She has this way of making little remarks that are painfully true, and I have often remarked, "Well, that's kind of true about Daddy and me; we are still struggling in that area."

I was much relieved when I read this anniversary note:

Mom and Dad,
Wow! 28 years later. What a beautiful example you both have been to Ben and me for your Spirit-led marriage. I only hope and pray I will have a marriage half as wonderful and influential and self-less as yours. I love you both more than anything in this world, and I've never felt unloved, or unsupported for a day in my life.

When I read this I thought about how I have done so many things wrong, which people who are very close to me know. I have many things I've confessed at the dinner table, things I've regretted. I've gone to my children and asked forgiveness for whenever I have failed them. I have also given them full permission to talk to a professional counselor about me if it's ever necessary. And I was totally serious about this possibility. I know that I have not been the perfect mom.

Ken and I have been teaching for years that a good marriage is comprised of two good forgivers. Twenty-eight years later that principle has kept our love strong. Forgiving freely is a life principle that Ken and I have seen blossom in Ben's and Jessica's lives—great preparation for their future marriages.

A Great De-Stressor

Have you noticed how a person gets a little snippy when he or she is under pressure? Maybe I should ask your spouse or kids how you act when you are under pressure. Recently during some jam-packed days, I noticed how Ken and I had been impatient with each other. While I knew that our behavior was not connected to some deep underlying marital problem, I did recognize the impatient "snippiness" as a stress indicator. Then I began to consider a possible de-stressor. I knew that I could not give Ken more hours in his day—or even a day off—but then the Lord brought an idea to my mind. I needed to look for an opportunity to be more of a servant to Ken rather than a servant of my demanding agenda. I noticed that when I stopped what I was doing and did a simple act of service for Ken, he not only seemed less stressed, I actually experienced some de-stressing of my own soul. The Word of God says that I am refreshed when I take the time to refresh someone else (Proverbs 11:25). As a wife and mother, serving is life-breathing, and there are ways to go the extra mile for someone you love that will not only de-stress them, but also be oxygen for your own soul.

After practicing a more creative servanthood, I came across the following excerpt from *Incompatibility: Grounds for a Great Marriage,* by Chuck and Barb Snyder:

> One of the greatest hindrances to a happy, successful, fulfilling marriage relationship is found in the word *expectations.* We bring into marriage so many preconceived ideas of what an ideal wife or husband should do. When our mate disappoints us and does not fulfill these expectations, little blocks of resentment over time start to build a wall between the partners. The greatest contribution to a happy, successful, fulfilling marriage relationship is found in the word *serving.*

When I read that the greatest contribution to my marriage is serving, I had a fit because I had just tried some creative serving as a de-stressor and it had worked! You may be thinking, *I am already a servant of my spouse.* Well, so have I been for 30 years, but this is a creative service, not the expected spousal service.

Application: The Stamp of the Adapting Spouse

Mentor Boaz

This Christmas, money was sparse and our children were concerned about not having enough money saved to purchase Christmas gifts for both Mom and Dad. Ken came up with a creative alternative for his gift. He asked our children to think of a memory that involved only Daddy and to write about the memory and illustrate it with a picture. Ben and Jessica really impressed us with their creative touch as they wrote and illustrated their memory of "Daddy and Me." I am so grateful for a husband who has so consistently spent quality time with our children, creating memories for a hundred Christmas gifts.

Adapting to Ken

Recently, in a men's meeting get-acquainted activity, the men were instructed to introduce themselves and tell what their hobby was. As Ken sat and listened to each man introduce himself and tell his hobby, he thought about his own hobby. Though he thought he might sound silly, he proceeded to share his thoughts, and said, "Hi, I'm Ken Kendall, and my hobby is my family. Whenever I have free time, I'd rather be with my family than anyone or anything." Well, the guys were probably not too impressed, but I can assure you there are three people who were totally impressed with his response—Ben, Jessica, and me!

> *How to remain whole*
> *in the midst of the distractions of life;*
> *how to remain balanced,*
> *no matter what centrifugal forces*
> *tend to pull one off center:*
> *how to remain strong,*
> *no matter what shocks*
> *come in at the periphery*
> *and tend to crash the hub*
> *of the wheel ...*
> *Perhaps a first step,*
> *is in the simplification of life,*
> *in cutting out some of the distractions.*

This excerpt from Anne M. Lindbergh's *Gift From the Sea* is such a gentle reminder. Amidst our busy schedules, there is one simple reality that can put everything into perspective: "For the LORD takes delight in His people" (Psalm 149:4). Cutting out some distractions, making room for His pleasure with me—that's my plan!

Ken's Desert Storm

Driving Ken to the airport early this morning, I had tears in my eyes because I knew Ken was concerned about the "storm" he was getting ready to face. The mission trip to Reynosa had escalated from a few problems into a full-scale storm. The border guards would not allow our trucks (which contained all our building materials) into Mexico, busloads of anxious teens and youth pastors were waiting, and political red tape was blocking the entrance. Before Ken even arrived, he received many frantic phone calls explaining the chaos. Amidst all this confusion, the project coordinator for Mexico quit! So Ken was flying into a stormy situation, and as we got closer to the airport, I said to Ken, "If I could only have one person at my side in a storm, I can't think of anyone I would rather have with me than you."

When I got home, the kids were still asleep. As I was reading my Bible, the proverb for the day affirmed my last statement to Ken. "Better a patient man than a warrior, a man who controls his temper than one who takes a city" (Proverbs 16:32). I got so excited when I read this verse. The Lord said, "Jackie, the chaos at the border of Mexico does not need a warrior/Rambo, but a patient man like Ken."

When Ken got on the plane, he opened his One Year Bible, and he, too, saw the verse in Proverbs 16:32. The Lord assured Ken he was the man for this "desert storm." When the kids woke up that morning, I shared this verse with them. We began to pray that just as God parted the Red Sea for the children of Israel, He would cut through the red tape at the Mexican border to free His children to serve Him in Reynosa. That very night, the first truck crossed the border! Yeah, King Jesus!

Partner in Parenting

Benjamin turned 14 on October 20, and Ken reserved a room at the Holiday Inn that weekend for a special father-son time together. This time was set aside for Ken to give Ben the blessing that every child hungers for (described in detail in the wonderful book *The Blessing,* by Gary Smalley and John Trent). During their time together, Ken not only spoke a blessing over Ben concerning his future, but also gave him a special challenge to remain sexually pure until he is married. At the end of the weekend, Ken presented Ben with a framed copy of the Scripture he used in declaring a blessing on Ben and his future. That framed Scripture now has a place in Ben's room as a visual reminder of their special father and son weekend.

Ken has been giving a blessing to both our children for as long as I can remember (attaching high value to them, giving meaningful touch, loving them unconditionally). As Ken effectively fathers our children, it has allowed both of us to grieve the reality of our never having received the blessing from our own fathers. Jesus has taught us to face the blessing we never received rather than denying it. By facing the loss of the blessing of our fathers, we can allow God to show us how to break this cycle.

In the vast majority of cases, parents who do not give the blessing never received it themselves. God has been such a good Father to Ken and me, we have learned how to give the blessing. I believe that the Lord wants to use Ken as an example of the Last Days prophecy that God gave through the prophet Malachi: "He will turn the hearts of the fathers to their children, and the hearts of the children to their fathers" (Malachi 4:6).

Timothy was mentored by a mom and a grandmother and then a surrogate spiritual father, Paul. Paul the apostle had an awesome "son in the Lord" who was mentored by mom and grandma—readying him for Paul. I have been loved by many spiritual surrogates as I grew spiritually. But I praise God that Ken and I have both been able and willing to mentor our own children.

Husband of the Year

The day before the memorial service for my brother, Ken stayed at home to handle all the calls while I was with my mom and family. That evening when I got home, Ken looked like he had been hit by a truck! I asked Ken if he was OK, and he said, "The reason I look so bad is because I have spent the whole day handling weeping women on the phone and those who came to our house." He went on to say that he cried with several of the women. How grateful I am that I am married to a man who knows how to weep with those who weep. One of the women told me that she was overwhelmed by Ken's tears and compassion. Ken's response reminded me of Jesus: "We do not have a high priest who is unable to sympathize with our weaknesses" (Hebrews 4:15).

Back-to-Back Serving Jesus

Ken drove me to Joe Robbie's Stadium where I would be joining some of the wives and girlfriends of the Marlins baseball team for a Bible study. We ended up in a sky box where the women invited Ken to stay while I taught a session on "The Incubation of Anger." Ken contributed ideas from the male perspective. After the Bible study, I was trying to witness about Jesus with two women. As

I was answering their questions and sharing how they could know Jesus personally, Ken and I were sitting back to back. Ken began witnessing with one of the young women, and as I was talking, I could hear Ken telling her how she could receive Jesus as her Savior right now.

I got so excited when I heard Ken begin to pray with the young woman that I almost couldn't finish sharing Jesus with the two women with whom I was talking. What a tag team Ken and I have been since we began serving together in a West Palm Beach youth group 25 years ago!

A Most Precious Bouquet of Flowers

Two days before Valentine's Day, Ben came to me and asked me for the location of a good florist. I smiled and asked, "Who do you want to buy flowers for?" He immediately responded: "Jessica." I told him that he did not need to go to a costly florist; he could simply go to our grocery store. Ben said, "Those are not good enough; I want to get Jessica something awesome." Well, I could not talk Ben out of this brainstorm, and I was honestly captivated and overwhelmed by another demonstration of Ben's love for his little sister. When Ben purchased the flower arrangement, he wanted to buy the best. The arrangement also included a beautiful ceramic box that she now uses for her rings. The owner (who knows Ken and me) knew that Ben's last name was not Vanderbilt, so she very carefully talked Ben into a little less expensive arrangement. The owner saw us a week later and told us what Ben had originally wanted to spend. Ken and I were so touched by Ben's heart toward Jessica.

Don't Worry; You'll Get Used to Her

A couple years ago, when I did something crazy, Ben laughed, but Jessica rolled her eyes in embarrassment! After Jessica verbally expressed what her eyes had communicated, Ben said to her, "Jessica, the older you get, the more you will get used to Mom and eventually find her funny." Well, Jessica turned 15 on Saturday, and I have seen the fulfillment of Ben's "prophecy." She has matured enough to enjoy her lunatic mom. Yahoo!

Another sign of her growing up was last Monday night, she and her daddy went out to dinner together for a special evening of challenge and blessing. Ken talked to Jessica about her making a pledge to sexual purity as she looks forward to the coming years of dating (not till she is 16, of course). He shared with her specific Scriptures (Psalm 45:9, 13 and 1 Thessalonians 4:3-4). After they went over the Scriptures, Ken presented Jessica with a ring that would be symbolic of her commitment to purity. The ring is a circle of gold hearts surrounded by silver. This special evening between Ken and Jessica caused me such tears of joy. Ken has always handled Jessica like such a princess. In fact, he presented the ring to Jessica in a beautiful glass slipper.

When I was a teenager, I used to dream about the ideal father since I had a difficult one. God has used the precious relationship between Ken and Jessica to bring healing to my wounded heart. "Do not be afraid; you will not suffer shame. Do not fear disgrace; you will not be humiliated. *You will forget the shame of your youth*" (Isaiah 54:4, italics added).

A Mentor Like Dad

Ben is being "mentored/discipled" by a man named Bob
Wharton. One day I asked Ben, "Why did you ask Mr.
Wharton to mentor you?" Ben's immediate response was:
"Mr. Wharton is a great Christian, he loves his wife, and he
is a good father—and those are the three things I want to
be." I was so thrilled with Ben's answer because I know
that his daddy set the first example, and now Jesus has
affirmed the things Ken has lived and spoken through
another godly man. Recently, when I asked Ben a hard
question about his dating life, he said, "Mom, Mr. Wharton
asks me that question every time we get together."
Yahoo! Thank You Jesus for perfecting the work You
begin in us!

Such Extravagant Loving

Outsiders may have considered Ben's birthday gift for his
girlfriend's 18th birthday a little extravagant. Ben took
every dime he had and purchased a watch for her, and he
also threw her (with the help of his party-animal mom)
a big surprise party. Such extravagant giving caused his
girlfriend to cry and later tell her mom that she feels so
unworthy of such love. As I was pondering whether or not
Ben was a little too extravagant—the doorbell rang and
I was greeted with flowers from Ken (who was in
Minnesota at a staff conference), and the card he sent with
the flowers said, "Just because you are special. Love, Ken."

As I carefully placed the flowers on our dining room
table, I realized that our son was behaving just like his
father. Ken has spoiled me with cards, flowers, and gifts for
the last 24 years. Ben is just following his dad's example.

For those of you who are raising sons without fathers in the home, be assured that your son's heavenly Father can teach him how to love extravagantly as a husband is commanded in Ephesians 5. Ken rarely saw his dad when he was growing up, so he leaned upon the Lord and the Word for modeling the love a man should have for a woman. When Ken and I were dating, I would discuss with other people the wonderful and thoughtful things Ken always did for me. An older married man said, "He's good to you because he is courting you—he'll change when you are married!" Boy, was he wrong!

Incompatibility: Grounds for a Great Marriage

Twenty-five years ago when Ken and I decided we wanted to be married at Christmas time (December 21), several people warned us against such poor timing. How cool to think today, 25 years later, we celebrate our anniversary during a season that focuses on the One who has been the superglue in our marriage.

Recently, when Ken came in from his men's Bible study, he walked toward me with his arms wide open and gave me the biggest hug. Then he said, "Jackie, I know why we have a good marriage 25 years later—because we are both actively seeking Jesus and we both know how to forgive freely." He had just listened to a man describe a horrible fight he had with his spouse over a seemingly trivial matter. He recognized that the magnitude of the fight was a reflection of the depth of unforgiveness between them. Ken proceeded to say, "You and I could be just as bitter and stuck in unforgiveness as this couple." Through the constant encouragement of God's Word, Ken and I have learned that through generous forgiveness, incompatibility is still grounds for a great marriage.

Vacuum Cleaner and Briefcase

One morning I saw Ken carrying our vacuum cleaner out the front door, then he came back for his briefcase and a bag containing cleaning supplies and work clothes. I asked Ken what in the world he was doing. "I am going to clean our World Servants office, because our new staff member arrives tomorrow, and I want it to look as good as possible." My heart was so touched by the fact that Kenny did not see cleaning the World Servants office (including the bathroom) as beneath him.

As I thought about his servant attitude, I immediately thought of Jesus and His coming to earth. Talk about humbling servanthood, from a smelly stable to a dusty carpenter's shop to meals with people whose souls needed major cleaning. In fact, in comparison to heaven, earth might have been like a big bathroom that needed cleaning. Ken has always had such a servant's heart, not only on the mission field, but also at home. The Bible commands a wife to respect her husband (Ephesians 5:33). Such humble, servant's behavior continues to leave me in "awe" of my husband. Of course, Ken is not comfortable with his wife bragging on his "servant heart," but I cannot constrain myself—I am challenged by his example more than words can express.

Spring Break Grace

Three weeks ago, we had the privilege of having two seniors from Liberty Baptist University spend their spring break with Ken and me. I had prayed that it would be a week where we would be a blessing to these young women whose heart passion is to make a difference in the world for Jesus. What happened after a week at the Kendall home? I'll let the girls' thank-you note tell you: "Ken, it is so great to meet a man of God that is so real! Truly you have shown me a true and real person who God is in so strongly. It is so wonderful to see the marriage you and Jackie have and be encouraged to have that, one day!"

Ken had to leave after two days and I had the privilege of a whole week loving on these precious girls. They asked me so many questions and so many of my responses had to do with grace rather than irrelevant minutiae. When the girls arrived back at school, Alli emailed me and summarized what the girls got from their time with me: "We miss you so much Jackie and we cannot stop talking about grace since we returned…we didn't know how amazing grace could be!"

An Early Father's Day

Recently Jessica sent the following message to her dad through a card she found:

Dad, as I was growing up, you always made my world feel safe. The deep calm of your voice steadied me…and the strong circle of your arms shielded me. I never felt vulnerable. As I got older, though, it dawned on me that the world you faced every day was a lot bigger and scarier than the one you had created for me. And I wondered, sometimes, if you felt like relying on someone else's strength for a change (the Lord was your strength)….

Now that I'm an adult and living on the outside of your safety net (I'm now in His safety net), I finally understand what sacrifices you made to make sure my world felt all right all the time. Growing up in the sanctuary of your love is something I will always cherish and a memory I could never forget. Now more than ever, I appreciate you for that. I love you, Dad.

When Ken read that card to his brother, his sister-in-law, and me, his brother said, "What was the occasion?" I smiled knowing that expressing gratitude is something our children know to express with or without a special occasion!

Whole Dreams, Broken Dreams

Our son was supposed to be getting married two weeks from tomorrow, but the engagement was broken after Ben went to a Christian counselor who asked him, "What do you want in a marriage?" Ben replied: "I want a marriage like my parents have." The counselor asked Ben, "Can you have such a marriage with your fiancée?" The answer was so hard; with tears he said, "No."

The rest is a very painful reality, but it was the worst best decision of Ben's life to have the courage to break the engagement three months from the wedding date. He is going through a great growth spurt spiritually and we are thrilled—broken dream makes way for a better dream.

Questions: For Individual Reflection or Group Study

1. Discuss this definition of *submission*:"Laying down the terrible burden of always needing life on one's terms."
2. What perception of the word *submission* were you raised with? (Ephesians 5:21-22)
3. Discuss the passage in Genesis 2:18 and the expression: *suitable helper.*
4. Consider the Hebrew definition of suitable: *"one like but facing the opposite."* Discuss the impact of needing to live unselfishly with your opposite, your spouse. (Philippians 2:3-8)
5. What is the most difficult aspect of adapting to your spouse?
6. Have you ever considered that self-control meant voluntary limitation? (Galatians 5:22-23; Titus 2:4-5)

Appendix

BOOKLIST
for Mentoring

 **Principle:
To mentor, you must
first be mentored.**

I am the sum total of all I have read. For the last 28 years,
I have been taught and mentored by some of the greatest Christians that have ever lived. How did I arrange
such a privilege? Through their writings.

The following list of books contains just some of the best
of all those heart-to-heart moments I had in my kitchen, reading the heart of some precious believer. Whenever I had
a particular need as a woman, wife, mother or friend, I would
visit my local Christian bookstore looking for another book
and another chance to visit in my kitchen with a godly
brother or sister.

These books were never substitutes for a consistent, daily, growing relationship with God through His Word; instead, they were just supplements to my discipleship. Just think, God's Word is God's heart in print, so the best way to discover what makes a certain Christian leader passionate is by reading their books and getting glimpses at their hearts. Those glimpses challenge me to follow Jesus as they followed Him.

Bible Study Helps
- *Hebrew-Greek Key Word Study Bible* (NIV) (expensive but great investment)
- One Year Bible format—for consistency in daily reading
- Different translations and paraphrases of the Bible: Phillips, Amplified, New International Version, The Message, and the New Living Translation
- *Strong's Exhaustive Concordance* (for looking up words in the original language of Hebrew and Greek)
- Journal to record the daily nuggets you receive (Isaiah 50:4) (Visit www.JackieKendall.com to see a year's worth of nuggets I have journaled.)

Trust Building
- *Trusting God: Even When Life Hurts*, by Jerry Bridges
- *Disappointment with God*, by Philip Yancey
- *In the Eye of the Storm*, by Max Lucado
- *Finding God*, by Larry Crabb
- *Through Gates of Splendor*, by Elisabeth Elliot
- *Passion & Purity*, by Elisabeth Elliot
- *Shattered Dreams: God's Unexpected Path to Joy*, by Larry Crabb

- *A Tale of Three Kings: A Study in Brokenness,* by Gene Edwards

Prayer
- *What Happens When Women Pray,* by Evelyn Christenson
- *Fresh Wind, Fresh Fire: What Happens When God's Spirit Invades the Hearts of His People,* by Jim Cymbala
- *Handle with Prayer,* by Charles Stanley
- *A Hunger for God: Desiring God through Fasting and Prayer,* by John Piper

Devotion to God
- *A Chance to Die: The Life and Legacy of Amy Carmichael,* by Elisabeth Elliot
- *My Utmost for His Highest,* by Oswald Chambers
- *The Christian's Secret of a Happy Life,* by Hannah W. Smith
- *Abba's Child: The Cry of the Heart for Intimate Belonging,* by Brennan Manning
- *Celebration of Discipline,* by Richard J. Foster
- *Pursuit of God,* by A. W. Tozer
- *Knowing God,* by J. I. Packer
- *31 Days of Praise,* by Ruth Myers
- *How to Overcome Loneliness,* by Elisabeth Elliot
- *100 Christian Women Who Changed the Twentieth Century,* by Helen Kooiman Hosier
- *Don't Waste Your Life,* by John Piper
- *Ruthless Trust: The Ragamuffin's Path to God,* by Brennan Manning

Faithfulness

- *Waking the Dead: The Glory of a Heart Fully Alive,* by John Eldredge
- *When Godly People Do Ungodly Things: Arming Yourself in the Age of Seduction,* by Beth Moore
- *The Stronghold of God,* by Francis Frangipane
- *A Tale of Three Kings: A Study in Brokenness,* by Gene Edwards

God's Will

- *Found: God's Will,* by John MacArthur
- *The Normal Christian Life,* by Watchman Nee
- *True Spirituality,* by Francis Schaeffer

Grace

- *What's So Amazing About Grace?* by Philip Yancey
- *Ragamuffin Gospel: Good News for the Bedraggled, Beat-Up, and Burnt Out,* by Brennan Manning
- *Healing Grace: Let God Free You from the Performance Trap,* by David Seamands
- *Redeeming Love,* by Francine Rivers (novel)
- *12 Steps for the Recovering Pharisee (Like Me),* by John Fischer

Self-Image

- *The Search for Significance: Seeing Your True Worth through God's Eyes,* by Robert McGee
- *Shame and Grace: Healing the Shame We Don't Deserve,* by Lewis Smedes
- *Inside Out,* by Larry Crabb
- *The Blessing,* by Gary Smalley and John Trent

- *Boundaries,* by Henry Cloud and John Townsend
- *A Way of Seeing,* by Edith Schaeffer
- *L'Abri,* by Edith Schaeffer
- *The World According to Me: Recognizing and Releasing Our Illusions of Control,* by Sandra Wilson

Parenting

- *The Key to Your Child's Heart,* by Gary Smalley
- *Kids in Danger: Disarming the Destructive Power of Anger in Your Child,* by Ross Campbell
- *Parenting with Love and Logic: Teaching Children Responsibility,* by Foster Cline and Jim Fay
- *When You Feel Like Screaming,* by Grace Ketterman
- *The Treasure Tree: Helping Kids Understand Their Personality,* by John Trent
- *Families Where Grace Is in Place,* by Jeff VanVonderen
- *Parenting Isn't for Cowards,* by James Dobson
- *The New Strong-Willed Child: Birth through Adolescence,* by James Dobson
- *Wild at Heart,* by John Eldredge (a must for moms of boys)

Marriage

- *Incompatibility: Still Grounds for a Great Marriage,* by Chuck and Barb Snyder
- *The Two Sides of Love,* by Gary Smalley and John Trent
- *His Needs, Her Needs: Building an Affair-Proof Marriage,* by Willard Harley, Jr.
- *Toward a Growing Marriage: Rebuilding the Love Relationship of Your Dreams,* by Gary Chapman

- *Strike the Original Match,* by Charles Swindoll
- *The Five Love Languages: How to Express Heartfelt Commitment to Your Mate,* by Gary Chapman
- *Love Life for Every Married Couple: How to Fall in Love, Stay in Love, Rekindle Your Love,* by Gloria Okes Perkins and Ed Wheat
- *Foolproofing Your Life: Wisdom for Untangling Your Most Difficult Relationships,* by Jan Silvious
- *Intimate Issues: 21 Questions Christian Women Ask about Sex,* by Linda Dillow

Sexual Issues

- *Eros Defiled: The Christian and Sexual Sin,* by John White
- *An Affair of the Mind: One Woman's Courageous Battle to Salvage Her Family from the Devastation of Pornography,* by Laurie Hall
- *Every Man's Battle: Winning the War on Sexual Temptation One Victory at a Time,* by Stephen Arterburn

Marital Affairs

- *Torn Asunder: Recovering from Extramarital Affairs,* by Dave Carder
- *Love Must Be Tough,* by James Dobson
- *Hope for the Separated: Wounded Marriages Can Be Healed,* by Gary Chapman

Sexual Abuse

- *Outgrowing the Pain: A Book for and about Adults Abused as Children,* by Eliana Gil

- *Wounded Heart: Hope for Adult Victims of Childhood Sexual Abuse,* by Dan Allender
- *No Place to Cry: The Hurt and Healing of Sexual Abuse,* by Doris Van Stone

These are only some (probably 40 percent) of the books I have read during the last 31 years. I always ask key leaders, "What was the best book you read this past year?" I also have had a subscription to *Discipleship Journal* for 12 years. This magazine has many articles written by many contemporary giants of the faith. I read this magazine every month; it is like mining for nuggets of gold.

I present this list of books as a guide. You can follow me as I have followed those who are following our Savior. If you have any questions along the way of your pilgrimage, you may contact me at www.jackiekendall.com.

New Hope® Publishers is a division of WMU®,
an international organization that challenges Christian
believers to understand and be radically involved in
God's mission. For more information about WMU,
go to www.wmu.com. More information
about New Hope books may be found at
www.newhopepublishers.com. New Hope books
may be purchased at your local bookstore.